THE NONFICTION NOVEL

Robert Augustin Smart

UNIVERSITY
PRESS OF
AMERICA

LANHAM • NEW YORK • LONDO

University Press of America,™ Inc.

4720 Boston Way
Lanham. MD 20706

3 Henrietta Street
London WC2E 8LU England

Library of Congress Cataloging in Publication Data

Smart, Robert Augustin, 1952-
   The nonfiction novel.

   Bibliography: p.
   Includes index.
   1. Nonfiction novel. 2. American prose literature—
20th century—History and criticism. 3. Modernism
(Literature) 4. Shklovskiĭ, Viktor Borisovich,
1893-   . Sentimentalnoe puteshestvie. I. Title.
PS374.N6S6   1985   813'.081'09   84-22028
ISBN 0-8191-4200-X (alk. paper)
ISBN 0-8191-4201-8 (pbk. : alk. paper)

All University Press of America books are produced on acid-free
paper which exceeds the minimum standards set by the National
Historical Publications and Records Commission.

Dedication

To Lisa, who inspired, and Orpheus: for my
children.

Acknowledgements

I am grateful to Gene Fitzgerald for all the
time and work and, not least of all, the belief.
Also, Gerhard P. Knapp and Richard T. Cummings
are due a debt of gratitude for their usual
sagacity. I am indebted to Naomi Nicolas for
her tireless and wonderful work on the manuscript, and to my partner, Lisa.

TABLE OF CONTENTS

Preface

My purpose in this study was to describe the nonfiction subgenre as both a significant departure from the conventional realistic novel form and as an important development within American modernist fiction. Although such nonfiction novels as James Agee's Let Us Now Praise Famous Men and Norman Mailer's The Armies of The Night have become popular and, in the case of Agee's book, have even become regarded as American "classics," their specific importance as nonfiction novels and their relationship to the novel genre in general have never been critically appraised. As a result, while many critics and students readily acknowledge that there is a "nonfiction novel," few are aware of the important distinctions between the conventional novel and the nonfiction novel. Various misconceptions about this new form and its parameters are often perpetuated, even within the limited critical literature which is available, and little (if any) attention is given to the implications of such a "metafictional" subgenre. For example, the three major studies of the nonfiction novel in English, John Hollowell's Fact and Fiction: The New Journalism and the Nonfiction Novel, Mas'ud Zavarzadeh's The Mythopoeic Reality: The Postwar American Nonfiction Novel, and Ronald Weber's The Literature of Fact, consider Truman Capote's novel In Cold Blood a nonfiction novel, and the first two studies consider Capote's widely publicized remarks about In Cold Blood an appropriate starting point for a definition of the nonfiction novel. This is in fact not the case, for Capote's identification with the nonfiction subgenre is more unfortunate than it is useful, especially since In Cold Blood is a conventional novel.

Thus, this study describes the parameters of the nonfiction novel, especially its distinctive narrative development (Chapter one), and explores the resulting definition in three separate examples of nonfiction: Victor Shklovsky's Sentimental Journey (Chapter two), James Agee's Let Us Now Praise Famous Men (Chapter three), and Norman Mailer's The Armies of The Night (Chapter five). In addition, both Truman Capote's In Cold Blood (Chapter four) and Norman Mailer's most recent publication Executioner's Song (Chapter five) are considered in separate sections, ostensibly to clarify my distinction between the non-fiction novel and the conventional realistic novel.

The nonfiction novel has become a radical anti-pode for the traditional novel, questioning both its philosophical premises and its formal characteristics. Thus, any discussion of the modern novel is partial unless the questions posed by the nonfiction novel-ists are considered. Hopefully, the continuing dialogue on the fate of the modern novel has come closer to becoming whole in these pages.

INTRODUCTION

The acknowledgement of subjectivity as the mode through which the world is inevitably received and interpreted is in fact the only adequately objective account of the world.   Roger Poole

Nochmals, ich schreibe keinen Roman . . . Thomas Mann

*   *   *

One should not wonder that James Agee worked over five years to publish the manuscript for <u>Let Us Now Praise Famous Men</u>, nor that once published in 1941, it sold fewer than one thousand copies before being reissued in 1961.[1] From its publication, the text proved almost too problematic: for Agee who was constantly threatening to destroy it, certainly for the editors of <u>Fortune</u> magazine who originally commissioned it, and for contemporary critics especially, who were unable to place the novel within the traditional categories of novel criticism.[2] <u>Let Us Now Praise Famous Men</u> has been acclaimed, rejected, and most often ignored until 1961, by which time it had come to rest under the dubious aegis of America's radical past. Typically, Agee's book is regarded as a phenomenon of the restless decades of the Nineteen Thirties and Nineteen Forties, a "final resting place" for similar works of this period which unfortunately differed from the more widely accepted novels of Fitzgerald, Hemingway and Wolfe.[3] Perhaps because <u>Let Us Now Praise Famous Men</u> was consigned to archives of the American Left, few critics have seriously understood either the novel's uncharacteristic relationship to the American Thirties, or its unconventional and critical assessment of the novel genre.[4] Typical is Daniel Aaron's widely recognized study of the American Left, <u>Writers on the Left</u>, which only mentions Agee's text in a footnote, indicating that it "immortalized" the Southern sharecropper in a "memorable" study.[5] And Richard Chase, in his "classic" study <u>The American Novel and Its Tradition</u>, mentions neither Agee nor <u>Let Us Now Praise Famous Men</u>.[6]

Recently, American social historian Richard Pells was less cautious in evaluating the novel's importance when he said it was a novel "without precedent in the history of American literature."[7] Indeed <u>Let</u>

Us Now Praise Famous Men not only differs fundamentally from the rest of the literature of the 1930's, it is also a significant critical work about the American novel. Within the text, James Agee distinguishes his work from both the conventional realistic novel[8] and the documentary, the forms which dominated this particular historical period. In addition, Let Us Now Praise Famous Men provides a blueprint for a new subgenre of the novel form within it: the nonfiction novel. By altering the traditional relationship of the writer to the text, and thus clearly identifying the implied author with the narrative viewpoint, Agee produced a radical modernist response to the conventional novel. The nonfiction novel was one of the earliest modernist forms in American prose fiction and is still vital today. Let Us Now Praise Famous Men first broke away from the convention and described this new form within the novel genre in America. Agee's novel is still, incidentally, the most insistent and self-conscious example of the nonfiction novel in American fiction.

However, Let Us Now Praise Famous Men was neither the first nonfiction novel, nor was it the first to distinguish itself so clearly from existing conventional forms. Nearly two decades earlier, Viktor Borisovič Shklovsky, a member of the Russian Formalist group Opoyaz, published Sentimental Journey, a nonfiction novel-memoir of his activities during and shortly following the Bolshevik Revolution in the Soviet Union. Within the tradition of Russian prose, Sentimental Journey accomplished what Let Us Now Praise Famous Men would achieve within the American prose tradition nearly eighteen years later. Shklovsky's novel also distinguished itself from the existing conventional forms, in his case the memoir and the historical novel, and likewise suggested the need for a nonfiction prose form. Unlike Agee,[9] however, Shklovsky had already developed a broad, independent critical theory based on "defamiliarization" or ostranenie, which describes an evolution of literary forms such as the nonfiction novel from conventional forms. In fact, one major critic of the nonfiction novel refers specifically to Shklovsky's theoretical work in describing the development of nonfiction,[10] while in Terry Eagleton's recent seminal work on literary theory, Literary Theory: An Introduction, Shklovsky's critical work marks the beginning of modern literary analysis.[11] Essentially,

Shklovsky's theory proposed that new literary forms arise from a need to change conventional forms which no longer "defamiliarize" the world and things around us in order to help renew our critical perception of them. Defamiliarization ("making strange") is the function of art, Shklovsky argues,[12] and pressure to evolve new literary forms grows as the ability of conventional literature to defamiliarize decreases.[13] Thus, in addition to writing a nonfiction novel years before James Agee wrote Let Us Now Praise Famous Men, Shklovsky also developed a critical theory separate from his own novel, Sentimental Journey, which is useful for our understanding of the nonfiction sub-genre.

The first time that the nonfiction novel gained widespread critical exposure as an innovative prose form came, not after Agee's novel was published, but with the publication of Truman Capote's historical novel In Cold Blood in 1965, a full four years after the reissue of Let Us Now Praise Famous Men. In an interview with George Plimpton for The New York Times Review of Books, Capote claimed that he had written the "first nonfiction novel."[14] Capote also described what he considered the major characteristics of this "new" form in that interview, and a careful analysis of his argument shows Capote's "definition" of the nonfiction novel to differ substantially from both Shklovsky's and Agee's descriptions. A more interesting issue in this argument, though, is the point that Capote's "definition" describes, not the nonfiction novel as he claimed, but rather the conventional realistic novel; in fact, In Cold Blood is itself a conventional (historical)[15] realistic novel and not a nonfiction novel.

Thus, this study proposes that the first American nonfiction novel was not In Cold Blood, but rather James Agee's Let Us Now Praise Famous Men. In her article on Capote's novel, Diana Trilling has already raised this question regarding the two texts: "James Agee's Let Us Now Praise Famous Men . . . [is] at least as close to . . . proposing a new non-fiction form as Mr. Capote's In Cold Blood."[16] In addition, there is a real need to define the limits of the nonfiction subgenre, to distinguish it from the conventional realistic novel, and to describe how the nonfiction form developed within early texts such as Shklovsky's Sentimental Journey and Agee's Let Us Now

Praise Famous Men, as well as in more recent examples
of nonfiction like Norman Mailer's The Armies of The
Night. Finally, Mailer's recent novel, Executioner's
Song, is discussed, since its publication again
raised old questions about the nature of the nonfiction novel, and about its relationship to the traditional realistic novel. In fact, Executioner's Song
is clearly a conventional realistic novel and is not
a nonfiction novel.

Chapter one, then, includes a discussion of current criticism on the subject and provides a definition of the nonfiction novel; Chapter two explores
both the elements within Shklovsky's critical theories
which are relevant to the nonfiction subgenre and his
nonfiction novel Sentimental Journey; Chapter three,
the theoretical center of this study, discusses Agee's
Let Us Now Praise Famous Men as an example of the
nonfiction novel as well as an attempt to define the
new form; Chapter four considers Truman Capote's In
Cold Blood, distinguishing it from the nonfiction
novel, and showing its relationship to the conventional realistic novel; and Chapter five focuses on
Norman Mailer's Armies of The Night as a nonfiction
novel, and includes a discussion of Executioner's
Song in light of our description of the conventional
realistic novel. Chapter six concludes the study
with a summary argument on the nonfiction form.

Initially, this examination does not construe
any historical influence between any of the authors
who are discussed. While it is conceivable in the
case of Capote and Agee, certainly no connection can
be suggested between either Shklovsky and Agee or
Shklovsky and Mailer. They simply did similar work
in separate places and times. As for the relationship between Agee and Capote, although Capote never
explicitly discusses Agee's work or his acquaintance
with it, it is conceivable that as a Southern writer,
Capote would have had access, however perfunctory,
to Agee's work, since Agee was not as obscure in the
South as he has been in the rest of the country.[17]

One final point needs to be made concerning the
relationship of the nonfiction novel to the modernist
novel, other than that this issue will become clearer
as the discussion progresses. As a work of modernist
prose, the nonfiction novel certainly resembles many
other novels which fall into this particular distinc-

tion. However, unlike most texts which might immediately come to mind - Joyce's A Portrait of the
Artist as a Young Man, Peter Handke's Self Accusation,
Heinrich Böll's Ansichten eines Clownes, among them -
the nonfiction novel attempts to broach the fictional
universe and do the impossible: the nonfiction novelist utilizes the basic "fictional" mode of the novel
to order the experinces of the text but tries to
transcend this mode (to create a third mode?) by
metafictionalizing the entire process, often in a
self-conscious manner. Usually, he fails, but not
without first demanding the reader's reassessment of
the novel convention and of the reading convention
which accompanies it. Thus, while Stephen Dedalus'
diary at the end of A Portrait of The Artist as a
Young Man offers an unusual antithesis to Joyce's
fictional universe which preceeds it, the diary is
nevertheless a working, integral part of that universe and does not try to transcend it in the manner,
say, that Hersey's The Algiers Motel Incident or
Shklovsky's A Sentimental Journey would.[18] In a
sense, Joyce is still poseur in the novel.

NOTES

[1] Actually, only six hundred copies of the book were sold in the initial press run by the Houghton Mifflin Company of New York.

[2] cf. William Stott, *Documentary Expression and Thirties America* (New York: Oxford University Press, 1973), pp. 290-291.

[3] cf. Richard Pells, *Radical Visions and American Dreams: Culture and Social Thought in the Depression Years* (New York: Harper and Row, 1973), and Walter Rideout, *The Radical Novel in the United States, 1900-1954* (Cambridge, Mass.: Harvard University Press, 1956).

[4] With the noteable exception of Stott's work and Ronald Weber, *The Literature of Fact* (Ohio).

[5] Daniel Aaron, *Writers on the Left* (New York: Avon Press, 1961), p. 195.

[6] Richard Chase, *The American Novel and Its Tradition* (New York: Doubleday and Company, 1957).

[7] Pells, p. 246.

[8] A clear definition of the "conventional realistic novel" is found in Chapter One of this study.

[9] There are many parallels between Shklovsky and Agee, other than the fact that both men wrote nonfiction novels. Both men were also interested in popular literature and, interestingly, both were extremely interested in cinema. Agee, in addition to working as *Time*'s foremost movie reviewer for many years, also wrote a number of screenplays, including academy award winner *The African Queen* and *The Night of the Hunter*. In the 1950's, Shklovsky wrote a number of essays on the cinema, many of which are quite insightful for the Russian film, especially the work of Kolushov.

[10]Mas'ud Zavarzadeh, The Mythopoeic Reality: The Postwar American Nonfiction Novel (Urbana: University of Illinois Press, 1976), pp. 37-38.

[11]Terry Eagleton, Literary Theory (Minneapolis: University of Minnesota Press, 1983), p. vii.

[12]"[the function of art is to] impart the sensation of things as they are perceived and not as they are known: . . . to make objects 'unfamiliar,' to make forms difficult. . . ." Viktor Shklovsky, "Art as Technique," in Russian Formalist Criticism: Four Essays, ed. by Lee T. Lemon and Marion J. Reis (Nebraska: The University of Nebraska Press, 1965), p. 12.

[13]cf. Richard Sheldon, "Viktor Borisovič Shklovsky: Literary Theory and Practice, 1914-1930," Diss. University of Michigan 1966, pp. 75-109. cf. also Zavarzadeh, p. 4: "Innovation in narrative, as in the arts in general, . . . is largely a function of the pressures created by the new configurations of forces in reality which render the previous aesthetic forms incapable of effectively approaching new experiential donneés."

[14]George Plimpton, "The Story Behind a Nonfiction Novel," in Truman Capote's In Cold Blood: A Critical Handbook, ed. by Irving Malin (Belmont, Cal.: Wadsworth Publishing Co., 1969), p. 25. This article orginally appeared in the New York Times Review of Books, January 16, 1966.

[15]I am using the historical novel as opposed to the romance: primarily a novel whose subject is more topical and often follows an actual historical occurrance. cf. R. Chase, pp. 12-21.

[16]Diana Trilling, "Capote's Crime and Punishment," Partisan Review 12 (1966), p. 252.

[17]cf. Alan Cheuse, "The Return of James Agee," in New York Times Magazine, 16 December 1979, pp. 12-16.

[18]cf. David Henry Lowenkron, "The Metanovel," in College English, 38:4 December 1976, pp. 351.

CHAPTER ONE:
THE LIMITS OF THE NONFICTION NOVEL

All the length of the body and all its parts were
participating, and were being realized and rewarded,
inseparable from the mind, identical with it: and all,
everything, that the mind touched turned immediately,
yet without in the least losing the quality of its
total individuality, into joy and truth, or rather
revealed of its Self, truth which in its very nature
was joy, which must be the end of art, of investigation, of all anyhow human experience. James Agee

You can say that the material for any novel is
autobiographical, and you are also bound to say that
the material for the reading of a novel is also biographical; that the material is not only the biography
of the writer but also the biography of the reader.
Michel Butor

                    *   *   *

Historically, we may consider the nonfiction
novel the first significant form of modernist prose in
American fiction. Nonfiction becomes a personal record of our (via the narrating persona) phenomenological[1] transition into the modern age:[2] the "nonfiction novel reject[s] the conventional notions of art
as the creation of order out of chaos and the writer
as seer."[3] Here as in Europe, the novel genre matured
into the dominant literary form essentially because it
proposed a common, unified conception of reality, and
so reinforced the epistemological underpinning of the
Nineteenth and early Twentieth Centuries. This also
made the novel available to a large group of readers--
mostly bourgeois--and a sympathetic relationship
developed between this readership, which was constantly
growing, and the conventional novel, what M. Zavarzadeh
calls the "totalizing" novel:

> In the industrializing societies,
> the conventional totalizing novel
> is the most expressive and popular
> form.(5)

Because of its basically mimetic conventions (especially of narration),[4] the conventional realistic
novel became the dominant literary form, and since it

also reinforced a bourgeois, empirical conception of reality, it became largely dependent upon this audience for its readership.[5] Thus, the "totalizing" novel, here called the conventional realistic novel, creates for the reader a commonly held view of external reality which, democratically,[6] describes a view of the world which is both the most acceptable and the most recognizable to the greatest number of people:

> Through a complete interpretation
> of life, the classic [realistic]
> novel orders the chaos of experience
> and shapes it into a comprehensible
> whole endowed with purpose and gov-
> erned by laws that are discoverable
> by the rational mind. In doing so,
> the conventional novel imposes
> necessity and certainty on life
> and, to the comfort of its bourgeois
> reader, removes the anguish of the
> contingent.[(6)]

This literary process has been called "conscientious realism" by Damian Grant, as opposed to "conscious realism," and reflects a "shared reality": a "truth that corresponds, approximates to the predicted reality, _renders_ it with fidelity and accuracy; the truth of the positivist, the determinist, whose aim is to document, delimit, and define."[7] "Conscious realism," on the other hand, is a more individualistic, ultimately more modernistic process--based on the coherence theory of reality--wherein the "epistemological process is accelerated or elided by intuitive perception," and whose ultimate fictive universe "is not earned by the labour of documentation and analysis [like] the realistic novel but [is] coined. . . ."[8] Thus, the conventional realistic novel, in order to reflect and affirm the essentially Aristotelian bourgeois view of the world which supports it, organizes experience "casually in a linear plot, with careful exposition, logical development, and the strong closural effects of completeness, resolution, and stability."[(6)] And, these "closural effects of completeness, resolution, and stability" are not created through authorial impositions on the material in the text, but are rather presented as inherent qualities of an empirical, bourgeois world.

Thematically, the bourgeois realistic novel ex-

2

plores "the dreams and nightmares of the mercantile
ethic, of middleclass privacy, and of monetary-sexual
conflicts and delights of industrial society," and
these themes are portrayed in a manner which "presup-
poses a system of correspondences between private
experience and the facts of communal reality."(28)
Structurally, the most characteristic aspect of the
conventional realistic novel is its omniscient narrative point of view, and (in what is a complex form of
the omniscient narrative) its use of multiple points
of view or "centres of consciousness."9 This narrative
point of view was a necessary development within the
novel genre, since it is the most "accurate" vehicle
for constructing a "shared reality" which most readers
would experience and affirm. Typically, this realistic, omniscient point of view selects and arranges
details in the novel as they would best represent the
common reality which this literary form assumes, and
so the narrative "eye" "chooses the details that most
convincingly embody . . . [the novelist's] interpretation of the 'human condition' in terms of the solid
texture of everyday life and thus . . . [gives his]
fiction credibility and internal believability."(77)
A personal experience is thus "deindividuated" and is
changed into a commonly held and approved view of
external reality, rendered in the realistic novel
through an omniscient perspective which creates an
objective quality ("credibility") within the narrative.
The novelist's world becomes our own through the fictionalizing process.

Narrative point of view is also the most distinctive characteristic of the nonfiction novel; as a
modernist form of literature, the nonfiction novel
requires a subjective, clearly identified narrative
perspective different from the unidentified, omniscient
perspective of the conventional realistic novel. This
crucial change occurred in response to an epistemological change from the empirical universe of the Nineteenth Century to the subjective, phenomenological
view of the universe held by the intellectuals and
writers of the Twentieth Century. Since the work of
Einstein and Heisenberg, and in the historical after-
math of the First World War, "the war to end all
wars,"10 the common bourgeois view of society has become less and less unassailable, and a non-absolutist
conception of the world has become more and more
acceptable, perhaps necessary. In addition, the development of a "technetronic,"11 society, shaped

ultimately by advances in communication technology, forced an epistemological change from an empirical universe to a subjective and indeterminate one.[12] In the United States, especially, this sophistication of communications technologies produced "an information overload which gives such diverse and disparate views of reality that no single interpretive frame can contain them all and still present a coherent vision of experience."(7) Inevitably, we have come to perceive the universe as unknowable with any certainty, and we have become more dependent upon personal interpretation than was true for the Aristotelian universe reflected in the conventional realistic novel. Unable to rely upon the typical universe of the conventional realistic novel, the modern novelist was (and is) also required to abandon the conventional omniscient narrative, since the conventional narrative assumes a "shareable reality" which is no longer believable. Also, since the subject of the novel was no longer largely self-evident and accessible, the narrative focus of the modernist novel subsequently shifted to consider form as well as content. This change parallels a similar problem in communications theory,[13] and stems from the artist's concern that since his subject matter no longer has inherent "credibility, resolution, and stability," then the form which presents that indeterminate reality must also be legitimized, since it is one "reality" which the writer controls. This, as David Lodge explains,[14] is one major characteristic of modernist fiction and grows from the author's inability to know and "mirror" external reality as a sui generis entity. Robert Scholes has termed this category of modern prose "metafiction,"[15] and, M. Zavarzadeh explains, the "intense self-reflexiveness of metafiction is caused by the fact that the only certain reality for the metafictionist is the reality of his own discourse; thus, his fiction turns in upon itself, transforming the process of writing into the subject of writing."(39) This quality is shared by virtually all modernist prose (Joyce and Virginia Woolf, e.g.), but it does not yet represent an assault upon the conventions of the novel genre. Rather metafictionality in this context is a formal response to the changed universe of the modern writer.[16]

Within the broad category of modernist fiction, one of the most cohesive developments has been that of the French nouveau roman, perhaps because it was one of the earliest international modernist movements. More-

over, the specific relationship of the nouveau roman
to conventional realistic fiction parallels in many
respects the relationship of the nonfiction novel to
the realistic novel.[17] Both subgenres are modernist
forms of writing, both developed from the conventional
realistic novel, and so, since the nonfiction subgenre
has received less attention than the nouveau roman,
understanding the nonfiction novel in relation to the
French novel should help illustrate the differences
between the nonfiction novel and the conventional
novel, and help ultimately to describe and define the
nonfiction subgenre.

Both in the French nouveau roman and in the American nonfiction novel, the individual writer phrases
his response to the modern, post-Einsteinian universe
through narrative form and focus. The nouveau roman
utilizes (for the most part) a narrative perspective
called chosisme,[18] which focuses on objects--often
repeatedly--while at the same time the human involvement in the perception of this "objective" world is
decreased, often to the point of creating an apparent
narrative anonymity.[19] This narrative manipulation,
heightens the reader's awareness of the passage's
subjectivity, its "literariness"; i.e., the fact that
the material in the passage has been selected and
arranged becomes more noticeable. In Robbe-Grillet's
La Jalousie, for example, this repetitive imagery establishes a narrative observing center--an "I" per-
spective--which, although it is not identified, nevertheless is clearly present in the text, unlike the
omniscient, detached "pose" of the traditional realistic narrator. This point of view has been called the
"camera's eye,"[20] and as the reader becomes aware of
the selection and repetition that occurs in the novel,
he is also aware that the material is being organized
and structured from a discrete and subjective point of
view, even though the perceiving center is concealed.[21]
Thus, the universe of the nouveau roman is subjective
and ambiguous--not objective and empirical--[22]and
resolves nothing for the reader; rather it confirms
his phenomenological and existential part in the universe. The reader must decide and interpret the
materials and events of the novel from his own perspective without the benign approval of the traditional
narrative.[23]

While the nouveau roman is narrated by an excentric or deliberately concealed narrator, the nonfiction

5

novel narrator clearly identifies himself as the narrating and "acting" presence in the text. The nonfiction novelist shifts his focus from the objects of perception to the perceiver of those objects in order to emphasize his (the perceiver's) role in the ultimate shape of the novel:

> [In the nonfiction novel,] the perceiver and the perceived do not exist independently; the perceived is part of the process of perception, and both are a function of the active participation of the perceiver in life.(43)

Thus the nonfiction novel tends to have as much, and occasionally more subjective and "autobiographical" material than objective material in it, simply because the personal point of view is such a crucial and distinctive feature of that subgenre. The most conspicuous and insistent quality of nonfiction is the narrator's presence and identity, and the fact that he experiences all that is communicated to the reader. In both Viktor Shklovsky's _Sentimental Journey_ and James Agee's _Let Us Now Praise Famous Men_, for example, nearly as much time is spent describing the writers' personalities as is devoted to the subject material, leading one of Agee's first reviewers to accuse him of "insufferable arrogance."[24] While the _nouveau romancier_ does not identify the experiencing, and ordering consciousness in the novel, the nonfiction novelist does precisely the opposite. The nonfiction novel always contains an experiencing-narrating "intelligence" which selects and makes significant the events in the novel. For example, in _Let Us Now Praise Famous Men_, Part Three, "Inductions," Agee eulogizes each of the tenant farmers with whom he has stayed during the past weeks and when finally (in a later passage) he speaks of the eucharistic quality of his first meeting with George and Annie Mae Gudger, it is his consciousness which finds their lives significant. Indeed, part of the insistent tone of Agee's narrative, we suspect, comes from his assumption that we ourselves would not find these lives particularly significant or "shareable." The significant passage comes in the narrative where he attempts simply to describe the room where he first encountered the Gudgers, and (ten pages later) once he becomes conscious of the sympathetic distance[25] between himself and the reader con-

cerning the importance of this meeting, Agee aborts
his subjective disgression and returns to the description with the words:

> But from where I say "The shutters
> are opened," I must give this up,
> and must speak in some other way,
> for I am no longer able to speak
> as I was doing, or rather no longer
> able to bear to. . . . at best I
> can only hope to "describe" what I
> would like to "describe" as at a
> second remove, and even that poorly.
> . . .[26]

And so, while the nouveau roman specifically locates
and describes objects in its fictional universe but
maintains an anonymous narrating consciousness, the
nonfiction novel (especially Let Us Now Praise Famous
Men) shows us that the significance of the described
objects depends upon our individual perception of them.

A second important dimension of the nonfiction
novel which is shared by the nouveau roman is its inclusion of the writing process in the subject matter
of the text. In the nouveau roman, the excentric
narrative consciousness becomes a metaphor for the
novelist (or implied author[27]) himself, insofar as he
is the narrating, selecting, and arranging consciousness working from a specific historical nexus which is
also reflected in the novel:

> the so-called nouveaux romanciers
> . . . developed what John Sturrock
> sees as the distinguishing feature
> of the works of Robbe-Grillet and
> Claude Simon, namely narration by
> a "problematic first person [whose]
> narration is his own objectification
> of himself," and the abandonment of
> traditional forms of preterite nar-
> ration in favor of the present
> tense.[28]

Thus the nouveau roman, along with the nonfiction
novel and other forms of modernist literature, includes its process of becoming as a part of the subject
matter. By contrast, the omniscient narrative of the
conventional realistic novel assumes an ontological
and epistemological certainly about its own existence

and function. Because it describes an empirical and unassailable reality which is shared by the reader, the conventional realistic novel never questions its "right" to exist in that world.[29] As American New Critics have pointed out, it simply is one object among a world of sui generis objects and has its own existence quite apart from both reader and writer.[30] In modernist fiction, the empirical universe of the traditional novel has been destroyed in the transition to the modern age,[31] and the "credibility" of the new "introverted novel"[32] (which includes both the nouveau roman and the nonfiction novel) is no longer self-evident. The modernist writer's universe is subjective, ambivalent, and relative, and everything within it--including art--exists and has value only as a perceived object:

> In the nouveau roman, this atten-
> tion to physical objects, which
> are strategically repeated in the
> narrative, is founded on a pheno-
> menological assumption that the
> world as portrayed in the conven-
> tional novel is too orderly and
> too vulnerable to human interpre-
> tation. In the nouveau roman,
> critic David Lodge has pointed out,
> "what is purged is not so much a
> matter of invented characters and
> actions as a philosophic fiction,"
> or fallacy, which the traditional
> novel encourages--namely, that the
> universe is susceptible of human
> interpretation.[33]

Thus, the introverted novel exists meaningfully because its final identity is acquired through the reader's re-experiencing of the text. In the nouveau roman, two levels of perception are communicated to the reader in the aesthetic distance between him and the text: 1) an awareness that the objects in the text are arranged by a discrete consciousness, and 2) an understanding that the text itself is significant, that it is a part of the textual focus, and that it acquires a final fictive identity through the reading process.

The nouveau roman is self-reflexive and recreates within itself the writing process; the narrative

8

structure thus becomes the metaphor for that creation. This point is presented convincingly by John Sturrock, concerning Robbe-Grillet's recent novel <u>Projet pour une révolution</u>.34 Sturrock discusses the "intended design of a New York fire escape" (to escape fires), and its possible "unintended" criminal use within the theoretical matrix of the novel:

> Now this [potential] malefactor is, as we know, bent on the ontological crime of wrenching the natural world into line with his emotional requirements; <u>he is the would-be-novelist and the escalier de fer the support for his culpable ascent from the real to a fictive order of things</u>. [italics added]35

Sturrock's point is that the particular identity or function of the fire escape depends upon the design imposed upon it by the "malefactor," who is the reader. By extension, the existence of that fire excape (and so of Robbe-Grillet's novel) emerges during the reading process, as the reader "recreates" it. Although the plot and actual events of this novel are not critical for this argument, one can begin to see that Sturrock's point concerning Robbe-Grillet's fiction is significant. For, by arranging his deceptively empirical objects within an ambiguous and subjective narrative or fictional world, Robbe-Grillet recreates the fictional process with the reader, thus making the reader a "would-be-novelist."36 Since Robbe-Grillet speaks only of a hypothetical character who commits hypothetical (i.e., "fictional") acts, he also makes the reader an accomplice structurer ("would-be-novelist") who will fill in the gaps in the narrative from the expectations which are supported and intimated in the text. Later in the same essay, Sturrock considers the metaphoric quality of <u>La Jalousie</u>: in "the novel of that name . . . [what] lies on the other side of the glass is the <u>product not of observation but [of the reader's] imagination</u>. [italics added]"37 Robbe-Grillet forces the reader to make authorial decisions in order to synthesize the narrative into some kind of closure. Finally, Sturrock discusses Robbe-Grillet's use of certain words in <u>Project pour une révolution</u> which have a double meaning:38

[these words] have their textual

9

role in the novel, but they also
point outside it, to the subjacent
theory of fiction which Robbe-Grillet sticks to so rigorously. They
form within the language of the
novel, <u>a skeletal meta-language</u>,
<u>performing miniature acts of criti-</u>
<u>cism on the text as a whole</u>.
[italics added]"[39]

His point is clear: Robbe-Grillet's novel--and the
<u>nouveau roman</u> in general--recreates itself, and places
the reader into the role of the "would-be-novelist,"
forcing him to discern and extract personal signifi-
cances from the novel's ambiguous narrative world.
This is an essential function of modernist fiction.[40]

Although less directly, the same metafictional
quality is true of the nonfiction novel. While the
<u>nouveau roman</u> directly implicates the reader as a
"would-be-novelist" by obscuring the identity of the
experiencing and arranging consciousness, the nonfiction novel attempts to link text and reader as
partners. In the <u>nouveau roman</u>, the reader must
choose his own interpretation from the given events:
did a murder actually occur, is an affair actually
going on, what is the relationship of the narrator to
character A . . ., thus making the interpretation
which results from the reading process dependent as
much upon the reader as upon the novelist. The
reader's role in the final synthesis of the events of
the novel is crucial. Unlike in the <u>nouveau roman</u>,
the world in the nonfiction novel is presented first
as perceived by the narrator-character, who also
narrates much of his own personality; this enables the
reader to identify precisely the consciousness which
has shaped the experience within the text. One significant difference between the two forms, then, is that
narrative closure occurs outside the text-narrative
for the <u>nouveau roman</u>, while it occurs within the text-
narrative for the nonfiction novel. That is, the
signposts of "approval" which we rely upon for interpretation are given to us by the author/observer,
often in direct conflict with the conventional indica-
tors of "accepted" or "approved" interpretation. This
means that the thematic interpretation of the narrative
is largely determined by the reader for the <u>nouveau</u>
<u>roman</u> and by the author/narrator in the nonfiction
novel. In nonfiction, the reader has only two real

10

choices; either to enter or to refuse to enter into a
sympathetic partnership with the narrator/observer in
order to re-experience the events in the novel.[41] We
can, in our turn, approve or reject the author's interpretations. In either case, the reader is not
taken lightly as an accomplice in the writing process.
Both Shklovsky and Agee try to recreate the materials
and techniques of writing so that the reader can critically understand and assume his own discrete relationship to this process. Agee's frustrated insistence on knowing who his reader is at the beginning of
the novel; "who are you who will read these words and
study these photographs. . .,"[9] demonstrates the
importance of the reader in the final creation of the
novel. Agee is clearly convinced that his text will
be re-experienced by the reader, who will likely come
away with a "different" understanding of the novel
than Agee wished. This assumption differs greatly
from the "shared reality" of the realistic novel which
Damian Grant, for example, described. So, one major
element of the nonfiction novel which sets it apart
from the conventional realistic novel is that it must
contain a major, actual (not assumed) experiencing and
conscious narrator who conducts the point of view.
Under this narrative influence, the critical reader
re-experiences and thus re-creates the novel. In this
respect, the nonfiction reader should repeat the act
of creation embedded within the narrative.[42] And,
unlike the conventional "totalizing" novel, the nonfiction novel mirrors a reality constructed from the
author's personal experience within the text, and not
from an external reality which "ought" to reflect the
reader's own: here the two composing processes (reading
and writing) are identical. By comparison, the reader
of the nouveau roman does not engage in a repetitive
act, for he synthesizes data from the text on his own,
without reference to a similar sythesizing process
occurring within the text. During reception, however,
both the nouveau roman and the nonfiction novel attain
a similar degree of "objectivity," in that the reader
is given control over the final shape of the fiction
he creates.[43]

Before finally describing the essential traits of
the nonfiction form, we need to distinguish it further
from the conventional novel. The nonfiction novel
differs from the conventional novel in that its narrative point of view is more clearly homogeneous than in
the traditional form. While the traditional novel can

11

be narrated from several anonymous "centres of consciousness," or from any number of omniscient or
partly omniscient narrators whose relationship to the
text, characters and events is often unclear,[44] the
nonfiction novel emphasizes the fact that the textual
roles of novelist, narrator and character are identical. Thus, the specific interests and personality of
the nonfiction narrator, which are often obscured or
even deceptive in the conventional novel,[45] are always
clear. Secondly, as indicated earlier, the conventional realistic novel assumes a shared universe which
every reader can understand in more or less the same
way.[46] In the nonfiction novel, however, the only
valid universe is the one which is perceived by the
narrator-character, who presents a reality often different from the reader's. In fact, this personal
perception _must_ be different from the reader's, since
this is no longer the "shared reality" of fiction.
Thirdly, the nonfiction novel differs from most traditional fiction in that it is always metafictional,[47]
since it assumes neither a shared reality nor a self
evident, _sui generis_ existence within a shared reality.
Nonfiction prose draws attention to its differences
from other prose forms; each text records an individual
and _atypical_ experience which gains a fictional identity through the reading process. This is significant
because as the writer argues for the validity of the
novel, he also pleads for the identity and validity of
his own experience and existence within it. The author's insistence upon the individual quality of his
own experience collides with the typifying quality of
the fictional devices he uses, thus creating the
dynamic narrative tension crucial to nonfiction. As
Eugene Chesnick observed of Let Us Now Praise Famous
Men, from "the very beginning, . . . Agee had been
trying to demonstrate the reality of his own life."[48]
Finally, the nonfiction novel differs from the conventional novel in that it is tied to a specific historical event and time which is experienced by one or
more clearly identified people. The conventional novel,
although it might be based partially, even mostly, on
historical material, sooner or later abstracts this
specific material into a "typical" configuration in
order to affirm the basically harmonious world which
it shares with the reader. The author of the conventional realistic novel transforms personal and specific
experiences into typical ones to avoid becoming too
hermetic and thus losing the reader's interest. This
is how a "shared reality" is constructed. The nonfic-

12

tion novel, on the other hand, since it is based on an
individual perception of the world, insists on the
atypicality of events and affirms the personal reality
of the narrator-character. This is why, for example,
Agee's experience with the Alabama sharecroppers seems
so individual, so much his, while the experiences of,
say, the miners in Zola's Germinal or of the blacks in
Harriet Beecher Stowe's Uncle Tom's Cabin are so widely
applicable and so easily stereotyped, even though the
emotions generated by all three texts might be similar.[49] And, at least in the case of Uncle Tom's Cabin,
this typical appeal to a wide readership was a deli-
berate aesthetic design within the text.[50]

We must also make clear at this point that the
historical novel and the documentary (especially in
the United States) are, despite the different names,
essentially not different from the conventional novel
form. Both utilize actual historical material and,
in the case of the documentary,[51] try to remain as
faithful to historical "fact" as possible, but both
also utilize the conventional narrative fictionality
or "pose" of the traditional novel. The narrators of
these texts are no different than, for example, the
narrator of Dostoevsky's The Possessed, which is also
based on historical material.[52] The aesthetic distance between the author and the text in this case is
still great, while the nonfiction novel attempts to
narrow this distance. The point is that neither form
suggests that the narrating consciousness is also the
experiencing and fictionalizing presence, a necessary
component of the nonfiction novel. Whatever histori-
city or "fact" the realistic novel begins with is
finally overshadowed by its fictional quality.

Finally, the term "nonfiction novel" is a recent
one, and has become widely known as a critical concept
really since the publication of Truman Capote's In
Cold Blood in 1965, where on the dustjacket, the publishers announced that the book "represents the cul-
mination of his [Capote's] long-standing desire to
make a contribution to the establishment of a serious
new literary form: the Nonfiction Novel." However,
although Capote claims responsibility for having made
the term an active critical concept, "nonfiction" had
been a term of disapproval shortly before the publication of In Cold Blood. It was used by such critics as
Jacques Barzun[53] ultimately to underscore the difference between the traditional assumptions of art (which
Barzun implicitly approves as "correct") and a modernist

conception of art:

> For Barzun, the "non-fiction
> novel" is the result of the
> failure of the imagination of
> the literary artist to transub-
> stantiate the "raw materials"
> of life into the finished work
> of art.(73)

Only since the nonfiction novel has become recognized
as a modernist form of literature has it also been
considered a valuable critical category. And, since
the publication of Capote's novel, only three major
studies of the American nonfiction novel have been
written. The most recent, John Hollowell's Fact and
Fiction: The New Journalism and the Nonfiction Novel,[54]
is useful primarily because he explores the rise of
"New Journalism" in the United States and the impact
which journalists like Tom Wolfe and Hunter S. Thompson
have had on the development of American popular literature. Hollowell's point is that nonfiction writing
has become an important dimension of popular American
prose, which had hitherto been dominated completely by
conventional fiction.[55] The problem with Hollowell's
study is that once he has described the relationship
between "New Journalism" and the nonfiction novel
(pp. 63-65), he does not go on to define and describe
the nonfiction subgenre. In fact, Hollowell repeats
Capote's "definition" of the nonfiction novel (pp. 64-
65), indicates that it "represents no new literary
genre,"[56] but never completes his exposition by describing the nonfiction subgenre, or even by showing
how In Cold Blood is actually a traditional realistic
novel. Thus, having raised important questions about
the nonfiction novel, Hollowell does not provide the
reader with the materials to answer them.

A second important critical text, M. Zavarzadeh's
The Mythopoeic Reality: The Postwar American Nonfiction Novel, is far more useful to the student of nonfiction. In the text, Zavarzadeh defines the nonfiction novel as a.) a modernist form of literature and
b.) as an innovative narrative prose form. The book
carefully explores the social and epistemological
changes which preceded the nonfiction subgenre (pp. 3-
49), and then attempts to define the nonfiction novel:

> I have used the term "nonfiction

novel" as a descriptive, not
a normative, concept for the
genre of prose narrative whose
works are characterized as bi-
referential in their narrative
mode and phenomenalistic in their
approach to facts.(74)

By "bi-referential," Zavarzadeh means that the nonfiction novel has both personal and subjective material
in it, as well as actual historical and "factual"
material. In addition, Zavarzadeh correctly indicates
that the narrator is usually one of the characters in
the novel (p. 84-85). We find, however, three major
difficulties with Zavarzadeh's description of the
nonfiction novel. The first concerns his statement
that the "nonfiction novel moves toward a zero-degree
of interpretation . . . by empirically registering the
experiential realities."(41) This is simply not the
case, for the nonfiction novel records a subjective,
personally interpreted universe which is clearly asso-
ciated with the narrator ("actant") and the character
("actee"). Because the nonfiction novel no longer
attempts to "totalize" its interpretation of the human
condition does not mean that it "moves toward a zero-
degree of interpretation;" it simply means that the
author-narrator now acknowledges the fact that this
interpretation is his own and is thus personally credible and significant. Zavarzadeh's point here contradicts a later observation in his study which
correctly describes the phenomenological relationship
of the author (perceiver) to the text:

the way the external world appears
to [the nonfiction novelist] . . .
is affected not only by his past
responses and assumptions but also
by his expectations about the future,
as well as by such conditioning fac-
tors as his culture and language.
The perceiver and the perceived do
not exist independently; the perceived
is part of the process of perception,
and both are a function of the active
participation of the perceiver in
life.(43)

It is clear in this passage that the nonfiction novel
is not "noninterpretational."

15

Secondly, Zavarzadeh points out that the nonfiction novel is not a subgenre of the novel, but is a genre by itself:

> The nonfiction novel is a distinct genre, a unique mode of apprehending and transcribing reality, requiring its own particular set of critical assumptions . . . which has completely different epistemological premises than the fictive novel and other forms of prose narrative . . . . (57,75)

Zavarzadeh continues that we cannot speak of "probability of plot," "narrative suspense," "round and flat characters," "theme," "narrative voice," and an "implied author" in a "genre of narrative"(75-76) which is completely distinct from the conventional novel. If this were the case, however, then we could not speak of a nonfiction novel; some other genre designation would be required for any discussion of this form. Clearly, Zavarzadeh is overstating the difference between the nonfiction novel and the realistic novel. The nonfiction novel does utilize a prose narrative variation, characters,[57] an implied author convention, and clearly shares a metafictional quality with most modernist fiction. It seems clear also that the nonfiction novel, while it uses a different narrative form than the conventional "totalizing" novel, is nevertheless a subgenre of the novel form. Zavarzadeh's own use of the phrase "genre of narrative" indicates his tacit recognition that the nonfiction form is a subgenre of the novel, despite his insistence to the contrary. The nonfiction novel is a modernist development of the traditional novel.

Finally, and this difficulty stems in part from the previous point about the nonfiction novel being a distinct genre form, Zavarzadeh states that there is no conventional "'plot' . . . in the nonfiction novel; rather the 'plot' of the nonfiction novel is one with the author's donnée: he cannot change or modify it in order to convey a private vision through it."(80) This also seems to be an overstatement or error in judgement. The nonfiction novel does not utilize the chronological and objective linear plot of the conventional novel, but it does nevertheless have a subjectively arranged sequence of material--events and observations--which indicate some movement toward closure. Indeed, perhaps the clearest difference between the nonfiction novel and the realistic novel is that the events in the former are not arranged to agree with the reader's own sense of form: they are personal and unique. This is truer of Shklovsky's A Sentimental Journey and Mailer's The Armies of The Night than it is of Agee's Let Us Now Praise Famous Men, but even within Agee's subjective narrative, the reader can discern a plot movement: the text documents Agee's gradual coming to terms with himself through his observations of the tenant farmers and through his personal reactions to them. And at the end of the novel, a sense of closure emerges, for Agee clearly has synthesized his personal feelings about himself and his task, and he conveys this sense to the reader.58 Thus, the nonfiction novel does have a type of plot movement, does interpret material, does present facts from a subjective point of view, and it is definitely a subgenre of the novel form.

Perhaps the most useful recent analysis of the nonfiction novel is Ronald Weber's The Literature of Fact (Ohio), a discussion of "nonfiction with a literary purpose."59 Weber correctly perceives the nonfiction novel as a modernist reaction against the limitations of an ultimately Nineteenth Century novel form; in his words, the conventional realistic novel did not make the "world clearer," but had rather "limited it, made it less alive."60 In our own age, the linear, detached narrative of the realistic novel which moves from "beginning to middle to meaningful conclusion, was based on an 'innocence' about a continuous, coherent, decipherable universe."61 The serious novelist, then, "had no choice" but to move in the direction of nonfiction since it "seemed the most authentic literary response to the modern condition."62

Weber's description of the nonfiction novel form is also essentially correct: he argues that the novel is a "complex counterpointing of its two constituent elements, history and literature."63 The dialectual relationship between historical event and reporting the event within the novel form is critical to an understanding of the nonfiction novel; as will become clearer shortly, the overwhelming quality and urgency of the historical event justifies the novelist's abandonment of the traditional novel form. Weber is also right about the peculiar narrative tension in the non-

17

fiction novel, which grows from the writer's attempt to "fuse, and at the highest level, the roles of observer and maker, true both to the exploration of event as event and event as meaning."[64] Thus the autonomy of fact is preserved from the tyranny of the writer's self.

The major shortcoming of Weber's study develops from his attempts to describe Capote's In Cold Blood as a work of literary nonfiction. To do this, he finds it necessary to blur an important part of his definition; namely, that the nonfiction novelist must never allow his own interpretation and fictionalization of events and characters to become detached from his own text personality to become a traditional "fictional pose." Weber begins by saying that the writer of nonfiction, "like the writer of fiction, can take us deeply inside people and events and construct works that move beyond story and plot."[65] However, he "is finally restrained by his commitment to the facts,"[66] unlike the fiction writer. Later, in reference to Capote's novel, Weber reasserts that the nonfiction novelist "cannot 'invent' facts in order to penetrate his characters all the more or enrich the implications of the account."[67] Yet, Capote clearly did "invent" facts and clearly did "stretch the truth" to fit the story of the Clutter murders within his fictional universe, a point Weber himself concedes probably happened (p. 74), indicating that such inaccuracy is finally "devastating." But in the next passage, Weber dismisses this point by saying that these discrepencies "might seem of small importance for the book patently reaches beyond its factual grounding to grasp the reader in the manner of the novel."[68] The issue here is not that Capote "reaches beyond" the facts of the Clutter case, but rather that he detaches himself from those interpretive jumps and allows them to become part of the narrative "pose" of the text. Blurring the lines of a definition in this manner casts considerable doubt on Weber's entire argument, especially since he is ostensibly working to establish the credibility of the nonfiction subgenre. In the end, In Cold Blood remains in his estimation "a detached work of literary nonfiction."[69] As the following pages show, Capote's skillful rendering of the Kansas murder case falls short of being a work of "detached" nonfiction.

Specifically, the characteristics of the nonfiction novel include the following: 1) the nonfiction novel is a long narrative prose text which is a record of actual historical events; 2) these events have been experienced by one or more specifically identified narrators, whose nonfiction role as both characters and narrators is clear from the text. For example, in Let Us Now Praise Famous Men, Agee openly describes his narrative posture in the text:

> As for me, I can tell you of him [George Gudger] only what I saw, only so accurately as in my terms I know how: and this in turn has its chief stature not in any ability of mine, but in <u>the fact that</u> <u>I too exist, not as a work of fic-</u> <u>tion, but as a human being.</u> [italics added]70

In this passage, Agee recognizes the dynamic tension between the nonfiction narrator's insistence on individuality and the tendency of the fictional devices he uses to typicalize his experiences. This tension provides the narrative energy unique to the nonfiction novel. 3) The nonfiction novel tends to focus on the personality of the narrator-character, and so will usually contain much autobiographical material. This is not merely to help the reader understand the personality of the narrator-character, but also reflects the writer's need to justify and validate his own existence within the novel. 4) The nonfiction novel will usually have a consistent and dominant point of view, which will be either a) the point of view of the narrator as a character referred to in the third person, and where the narrator identifies himself as the character, or b) the point of view of a first-person narrator as character who often makes references to the time of writing and to the time of actual experiencing in the novel. Thus, both the roles of character and narrator (fictionalizer) are kept distinct.71 This dialectical balance helps maintain the tenuous equation between the individual experience and the fictional experience essential to nonfiction. 5) The nonfiction novel describes an individual, discrete world not shared by the reader. This is the primary reason for the subjective material in the text, as well as for the narrator-character's attempt to legitimize that personal reality. And finally, 6) the nonfiction novel usually has a clear metafictional quality. While trying to legitimize his experiences in the novel, the nonfiction writer also establishes the validity of the form he used to frame it. As the most immediate "reality" over which the novelist has control, the form of the novel and its differences from conventional literary forms become part of the narrative focus. This metafictional dimension is a major concern in both Let Us Now Praise Famous Men and A Sentimental Journey.

These are the distinctive features of the nonfiction novel, especially but not exclusively as it has evolved into an important American prose form. We need next to explore the subsequent development of the nonfiction subgenre first in the two texts which best reflect its development from the conventional novel, Agee's Let Us Now Praise Famous Men and Viktor Shklovsky's A Sentimental Journey, and then through the major novels of Truman Capote and Norman Mailer, the two American novelists who best represent the direction of the nonfiction subgenre since Shklovsky and Agee. Respectively, these texts are Truman Capote's In Cold Blood and Norman Mailer's The Armies of The Night and Executioner's Song. It is between these two poles that the nonfiction novel has matured and is now a legitimate, distinctive subgenre in American prose.

NOTES

[1] Phenomenological is used here in its most limited
sense: basically that the nature of reality has changed
from an empirical one to one which is made up of primarily subjective phenomena. In addition, the term
is used in the same sense as in the quote from John
Sturrock on page 7; cf. also M. Zavarzadeh, p. 57.

[2] Even well into the 1950's, the novel was described in the same terms as it had been since before
1900 by American critics, and this interpretation was
also supported in most if not all American colleges
and universities. cf. Bernard De Voto, "The Invisible
Novelist," in The World of Fiction (Boston: Little,
Brown, 1950).

[3] Zavarzadeh, p. 4. Subsequent quotes have page
numbers in parenthesis.

[4] This is the conceptual premise behind a critical
text such as Wayne Booth's The Rhetoric of Fiction,
for example, which is basically an extended typology
of narrative forms.

[5] cf. Ian Watt, The Rise of The Novel (Berkeley:
University of California Press, 1957), Chapters one
and two.

[6] This "democratic imagination" is characteristic
of a bourgeois society. cf. Lionel Trilling, The
Liberal Imagination (New York: Oxford University
Press, 1950).

[7] Damian Grant, Realism (London: Methuen & Co.,
Ltd, 1970), p. 9.

[8] Ibid.

[9] The term belongs to Henry James, and was used
first in an introduction or preface to The Ambassa-
dors. cf. Henry James, The Art of the Novel: Critical
Prefaces by Henry James, ed. by R.P. Blackmur (New

York: Charles Scribner's Sons, 1937).

[10] cf. Roger Shattuck, _The Banquet Years_ (New York: Dutton & Co., 1967), Ch. one.

[11] "A technetronic society is 'a society that is shaped culturally, psychologically, and economically by the impact of technology and electronics--particularly in the area of computers and communications." Zbigniew Brezezinski quoted in Zavarzadeh, p. 3.

[12] cf. Marshall McCluhan, _The Medium is the Massage_ (New York: Goddard University Press, 1969).

[13] Here also, the best record (and earliest, perhaps) of this immense change in communications theory is found in the work of M. McCluhan, esp, in _The Medium is the Massage_. See also Jürgen Habermas, _Communica- and the Evolution of Society_, trans. by Thomas McCarthy (Boston: Beacon Press, 1979).

[14] David Lodge, "The Language of Modernist Fiction: Metaphor and Metonymy," in _Modernism_, ed. by Malcolm Bradbury and John MacFarlane (Middlesex, U.K.: Penquin Books, Ltd., 1976), pp. 481-482.

[15] Robert Scholes, _Fabulation and Metafiction_ (Urbana: University of Illinois Press, 1979), pp. 108-109, 56, 127. "'Metafiction' is ultimately a narrational metatheorem whose subject matter is fictional systems themselves and the molds through reality is patterned by narrative conventions." Zavarzadeh, p. 39.

[16] Lowenkron, p. 353.

[17] cf. John Hollowell, Fact and Fiction: _The New Journalism and the Nonfiction Novel_ (Chapel Hill: The University of North Carolina Press, 1977), pp. 78-79.

[18] The term was first coined by Harry Levin, _The Gates of Horn: A Study of Five French Realists_. (New York: Oxford University Press, 1963), p. 452.

[19] This particular quality has been called the

"dehumanization of art" by José Ortega Y Gassett, and forms--for him--the characteristic quality of modernist art. cf. José Ortega Y Gasset, <u>The Dehumanization of Art and Notes On the Novel</u>, trans. by Helene Weyl (Princeton: Princeton University Press, 1948).

[20] cf. Norman Friedman, "Point of View in Fiction," in <u>The Theory of the Novel</u>, ed. by Philip Stevick (New York: The Free Press, 1967), pp. 130-131.

[21] For example, in a section early in the novel which compares the different manner in which A... and Franck eat with a spoon, the narrator contrasts the two: "Et, par opposition, il oblige à constater que "..., au contraire, vient d'achever la même opération san avoie l'air de bougermais sans attirer l'attention, non plus, par une immobilité anormale. It faut un regard à son assiette vide, mais salie, pour se convaincre qu'elle n'a pas omis de se servir. La mémoire parvient, d'ailleurs, à reconstituer quelques mouvement de sa main droite et de ses lèvres, quelques allées et venues de la cuillère entre l'assiette et la bouche, que peuvent être considérés commes significatifs." Alain Robbe-Grillet, <u>La Jalousie</u> (Paris: Les Éditions de Minuit, 1957), pp. 23-24. Obviously, the narrator here has a memory of A..., a sense for what is normal and habitual as opposed to what is not, and in the final line of the quote, indicates in an indirect but nevertheless clear manner what might be considered significant by someone who was observing A... and Franck from a less than disinterested position. This is the point of our argument.

[22] Incidentally, this change has been explored by a French <u>nouveau romancier</u>, Nathalie Sarraute, in her collection of essays entitled <u>L'Ère du Soupcon</u> (Paris: Gallimard, 1956).

[23] To some extent, this is true of virtually every fictional text, but is especially true of the <u>nouveau roman</u>. While the conventional novel--since it tries to mirror a reality which it and the reader will have in common-allow only minor room for active and sympathetic interpretation by the reader, the <u>nouveau roman</u> depends on the reader to synthesize it, to bring it to narrative closure.

[24] Stott, p. 304.

[25] cf. Wayne Booth, _The Rhetoric of Fiction_ (Chicago: The University of Chicago Press, 1971), p. 156. This is another indication within the text that the experiences in it are significant for Agee first, and for the reader only after the reception process.

[26] James Agee and Walker Evans, _Let Us Now Praise Famous Men_ (Boston: Houghton-Mifflin Co., 1961), p. 403. All subsequent references will be from this edition.

[27] Booth, 70-76: "As he writes, the author . . . creates not simply an ideal . . . but an implied version of 'himself'. . . .", p. 70.

[28] John Fletcher and Malcolm Bradbury, "The Introverted Novel," in _Modernism_, ed. by Malcolm Bradbury and James MacFarlane (Middlesex,U.K.: Penquin Books, Ltd., 1976), pp. 413-414.

[29] The fiction of Zola or the Brothers Goncourt especially comes to mind.

[30] cf. for example, René Wellek and Austin Warren, _Theory of Literature_ (New York: Harcourt, Brace & World, Inc., 1956), ch. 12, pp. 142-157.

[31] cf. Zavarzadeh, pp. 3-49.

[32] Fletcher and Bradbury, p. 394-395.

[33] Hollowell, p. 79.

[34] John Sturrock, "The project a A l'aine robe grillée," in _Directions in the Nouveau Roman_, ed. by G. Almansi (Canterbury, U.K.: Scottish Academic Press, 1971).

[35] Ibid., pp. 9-10.

[36]This is true of other Robbe-Grillet texts, notably Les Gommes where the detective novel becomes a metaphor for the fictional process, and in his shorter texts, La Chambre Sécrete, where the artistic process is recreated for the reader, or rather, with the reader.

[37]Sturrock, p. 10.

[38]"subjectiv (p. 39), anecdote (p. 54), phychodrame (p. 55), ouvrage (p. 78), essentiel (p. 85), fictif (p. 124), humaniste (p. 153) . . .", Ibid, p. 13.

[39]Ibid., pp. 13-14.

[40]This is the thrust of Fletcher and Bradbury's article on the modernist novel, and is especially important here since both the nonfiction novel and the nouveau roman are modernist forms of fiction.

[41]Recent perception aesthetics would argue that the reader is always a "partner" in the literary process, however unwilling or negative, so long as the text is read throughout. cf. Edwin Black, Rhetorical Criticism: A Study in Method (Madison: University of Wisconsin Press, 1965), and E.D. Hirsch, The Aims of Interpretation (Chicago: University of Chicago Press, 1976).

[42]As chapter three will show, Agee was very conscious of the reader during the time he was writing (1940-41), and sought to discourage a "conventional" reading of his novel, for fear that the reader's experience would be less intense than Agee's own, since he would be less aware and critical than Agee was himself.

[43]To a degree, this is true of any text, but in the conventional novel, the usually omniscient narrator invites a closer sympathetic relationship between the text and the reader, and implies that the world in the text is the world of the reader. The nonfiction novel does not trade on this assumption of shared realities.

[44]cf. Friedman, pp. 118-131.

[45]e.g., the narrator of Dostoevsky's The Possessed.

[46]A glance at 90% of popular American fiction
would confirm this point that the realistic novel has
remained virtually unchanged since the last century.

[47]cf. Viktor Shklovsky, O teorii prozy (Moscow:
n.p., 1929), ch. 2, pp. 27-61, ch. 4, pp. 131-162, for
a discussion of other conventional texts which are not
nonfiction novels, but which are nevertheless metafictional. e.g., Sterne's Tristram Shandy.

[48]Eugene Chesnick, "The Plot Against Fiction:
Let Us Now Praise Famous Men," The Southern Literary
Journal (1971), p. 63.

[49]The popular appeal and effect of this kind of
novel--especially Uncle Tom's Cabin--raise important
questions about rhetorical (i.e., as propaganda) role
of this popular fiction.

[50]Ante-Bellum: Three Classic Works on Slavery by
Hinton Rowan Helper and George Fitzhugh, ed. by Harvey
Wish (New York: G.P. Putnam's Sons, 1960), p. 3.

[51]cf. Stott, pp. 190-211.

[52]The Possessed is based on a terroristic incident in Moscow (The "Nechayev Affair"); Dostoevsky
obtained information about the incident from, among
other things, the newspapers and subsequently worked
these details into the text. cf. Konstantin Mochulsky,
Dostoevsky: His Life and Work, trans. by M.A. Minihan
(Princeton: Princeton Univresity Press, 1971),
pp. 311-314.

[53]Jacques Barzun, "Proust's Way" The Griffen 5
(1956), p. 6.

[54]John Hollowell, Fact and Fiction: The New

Journalism and the Nonfiction Novel (Chapel Hill: The University of North Carolina Press, 1977).

[55] Ibid., pp. 48-62.

[56] Ibid., p. 85.

[57] This is implicit in Zavarzadeh's own use of the terms "Actant" and "Actee" (p. 79), which seem to be merely substitute terms for "characters" and which could well be accommodated within the existing critical concept.

[58] cf. Agee, p. 470-471.

[59] Ronald Weber, The Literature of Fact (Athens, Ohio: Ohio University Press, 1980), p. 1.

[60] Ibid., p. 40

[61] Ibid.

[62] Ibid., pp. 40-41.

[63] Ibid., p. 2.

[64] Weber, p. 50.

[65] Ibid., p. 45.

[66] Ibid.

[67] Ibid., p. 79.

[68] Weber, pp. 74-75.

[69] Ibid., p. 159.

[70] Agee, p. 12.

27

[71]This also indicates an awareness on the author's part, e.g., Shklovsky, of his "implied author's" role, meaning that he understands that this experience would be different at a different historical point. The experience in the nonfiction novel is both one of re- cording and experiencing at one specific historical nexus. Hence, Shklovsky's references to both the time of experiencing and the time of recording in <u>A Senti- mental Journey</u>.

CHAPTER TWO

VIKTOR SHKLOVSKY AND A SENTIMENTAL JOURNEY

Criticism and invention are two faces, two aspects of the same activity.   Michel Butor

Only the creation of new forms of art can restore
to man sensation of the world, can resurrect things
and kill pessimism.   Viktor Shklovsky

*   *   *

Viktor Shklovsky's A Sentimental Journey (1923)
is important in the development of the nonfiction
novel for two reasons: first, Shklovsky wrote A Sentimental Journey following an important theory of
literary development and succession which he developed
between 1913 and 1929, along with his Formalist colleagues Boris Eichenbaum and Yury Tynyanov.   Thus,
both Shklovsky's theoretical and practical work are
crucial to our discussion of the nonfiction novel.
And secondly, A Sentimental Journey itself is significant[1] because Shklovsky structured it into two distinct sections and displays in each a different
aesthetic form.[2]   Part one, "Revolution and the Front,"
chronicles Shklovsky's activities during 1917 ("the
February Revolution, the Kerensky Offensive, the
Kornilov Revolt, and the occupation of Persia"[3]) and
is more or less a straightforward record of his activities and impressions at that time.[4]   Part two,
"Writing Desk," chronicles the years 1918-1922 and
"describes Shklovsky's underground activities against
the Bolsheviks, his escape to the Ukraine and service
under Hetman Skoropadsky, and his joining the Reds to
fight against General Wrangel in the southern
Ukraine."[5]   Moreover, part two is a parody of "Revolution and Front," which indicates that the line of
succession in this novel is from the conventional
realistic novel and memoir to the nonfiction novel.
In addition, although it was written very early in
this century, A Sentimental Journey fits well the description of the nonfiction novel provided in the
previous chapter.

Briefly, Shklovsky understood art as a rhetorical
category of human discourse, whose primary function

29

was to make objects "'unfamiliar', to make forms difficult, to increase the difficulty and length of perception because the process of perception is an aesthetic
end in itself and must be prolonged."[6] This process
of "making strange" of defamiliarization he called
ostranenie, and it is the basis for most of his critical work. _Ostranenie_ refers to the effect of those
devices in a literary text which, among other things,
prolong the perception process and, by so doing, force
the reader to see objects more critically, clearly,
and in a new and unconventional light.[7] The techniques which a specific author uses to make his subject "strange" are devices of _ostranenie_, and their
sum total in a work constitutes the "artistic" quality
or "literariness (_literaturnost_)" of that text. The
literaturnost of any work is determined by the author's
manipulations of the text by which he "defamiliarizes"
and presents conventional literary objects in a new
and striking manner. Shklovsky also understood that
ostranenie plays a role in the evolution of literary
genres. As one particular device is used over and
over, it becomes conventional and hackneyed; the
reader's perception of the objects in the text becomes
habitual or "automatic," and he responds to a literary
text as he would to a newspaper or to a familiar piece
of writing.[8] Forced to rely upon old, conventional
devices, the writer is no longer able to present experiences in a fashion which is new and personally
significant. The means of discourse, to use James
Kinneavy's term,[9] between the writer and the reader
ceases being effective.

At this point, according to Shklovsky's theory,
the writer or artist shifts his focus from the subject
of the text to the technical devices of writing. Once
a device has become "automatic" (conventional), and
no longer defamiliarizes, then it must itself be "made
strange," or defamiliarized. The literary process
which is used to defamiliarize the conventional device
is parody, and its ultimate aim is to point out the
need for a new form. This is how _ostranenie_ plays a
role in literary succession:

> parody is often a lever of literary
> change; by poking fun at a specific
> set of conventions which tend to de-
> generate into stale clichés the
> artist paves the way for a new, more

30

"perceptible" set of conventions . . . .[10]

Thus parody exposes the stale conventionality of certain forms and devices, opening the door for new and
different forms which will once again "increase the
difficulty and length of perception."[11] Moreover,
this development or evolution from one literary form
to another is not necessarily a direct one, as Shklovsky explains in O teorii prozy (1929): "In the liquid-
ation of one literary school by another, the inheritance is passed down, not from father to son, but from
uncle to nephew."[12] And as he explains in A Sentimental
Journey, most new forms emerge from other "peripheral"
forms which have either declined or which have never
been popular forms:

> New forms in art are created by
> the canonization of peripheral
> forms. Pushkin stems from the
> peripheral genre of the album,
> the novel from horror stories,
> Nekrasov from the vaudeville,
> Blok from the gypsy ballad,
> Mayakovsky from humorous poetry.[13]

Thus, for whatever inconsistencies and overstatements
in the rest of his theoretical work, Shklovsky correctly understood that the textual parody of hackneyed
literary conventions indicates the need for a new form.
For this reason, he found Lawrence Stern's Tristram
Shandy the "most typical"[14] of novels. The fact that
he deals with this particular novel in both an early
essay[15] and in O teorii prozy (his major theoretical
work) suggests that Sterne's work had a major influence on Shklovsky's. It is not surprising, then, that
the novel in which Shklovsky parodies a conventional
form and so paves the way for the nonfiction novel is
named after Lawrence Sterne's own memoirs: A Sentimental Journey.

As mentioned, A Sentimental Journey is divided
into two sections, each quite different from the other.
The first, "Revolution and the Front," is loosely a
memoir, but only loosely, for even here Shklovsky
seemed dissatisfied with that form as it had been used
by his contemporaries, (e.g., Henri Barbusse in Le Feu,
1916),[16] and began to experiment with it. The most
apparent difference between Shklovsky's novel and the
conventional memoir is his use of a disjointed episodic

31

structure in lieu of a more conventional chronological
structure. There is a chronology of sorts in the narrative, because Shklovsky repeatedly informs the
reader of the time and place which he is writing:

> I'm writing on July 22, 1919. (75)

> And now it's July 30, 1919, and I'm
> writing while on guard with a rifle
> between my legs. (80)

> I'm now writing at midnight on
> August 9. (106)

> I'll stop writing.   Today is August
> 19, 1919.   (130)

But this sketchy chronology does not really organize
the narrative; it is important only because it draws
attention to the writing process, a point which
Shklovsky wishes to emphasize. Shklovsky organizes
events and experiences thematically or by motifs in
the narrative, rather than chronologically, and he
thus underscores these events by repeating and ex-
plaining those which appear most important to him.
For example, near the end of "Revolution and the
Front" and the tale of his exploits in Persia, Shklovsky writes:

> Thus transpired and thus ended the
> Russian anabasis, or rather kata-
> basis--the withdrawal of several
> tens of thousands of men, traveling
> exactly like the companians of
> Xenophon along the routes of Kur-
> distan and, moreover, also traveling
> with elected leaders. Whether or
> not the Kurds are descendents of
> Xenophon's Carduchi, their customs
> have remained the same. But the
> spirit of warriors that force their
> way home changes. Perhaps everything
> can be explained by the fact that
> Xenophon's warriors were warriors by
> profesion and our - soldiers of mis-
> fortune. (126)

In this passage, he moves quickly from the retreat to
an obscure point about the Kurds having descended from

Xenophon's army back to the retreat of the Russian troops, without sorting out the details carefully for the reader. The result is an impression that he selected and arranged the material by association. Thus immediately following this passage, he tells the reader (almost apologetically), "One more story, quite short." The point, obviously, lies not in the details but in his experience.

This is the way all of "Revolution and the Front" is organized, and the narrative seems designed to emphasize that this is Shklovsky's personal history and not an objective recounting of the events of 1917. As one of the keys to the nonfiction novel, this is an important development in A Sentimental Journey. Within the associative structure of the narrative, Shklovsky arranges most of the material around motifs, the most significant of which are the falling stone and the roof, and themes, the most important of which are the horror, insanity, and cruel degradation perpetrated by human beings in time of war. The motifs of the falling stone (developed mostly in Part Two, "Writing Desk") and of the roof are personal motifs which have become metaphors for the role which Shklovsky the character/narrator plays in the narrative, and result from the hopeless cruelty which he sees everywhere around him. Shklovsky begins a section entitled "Persia" in Part One with the following: "I begin to write again. I was writing about despair. I'll go on."(72) Then, in the course of describing the Russian army's activities in Persia, he relates the following story:

> Apropos of pity. . . .There's a
> Cossack. In front of him lies a
> naked baby, abandoned by the Kurds.
> The Cossack wants to kill it. He
> hits it once and stops to think,
> hits it again and stops to think.
> They tell him: "Finish it off."
> And he: "I can't- I feel sorry for
> it." (99)

Then in the very next line Shklovsky moves on to his arrival in the small town of Solozhbulak, without pausing to comment on the story he has just told. At first, this may seem cruel in itself, and the extreme detachment of Shklovsky-narrator seems to elicit more than a sense of irony, but the key to understanding

33

this and many other stories like it lies in the passage
above it: "When you take the roof off a house built of
clay and straw, the house simply turns into a pile of
clay. (99) This is Shklovsky's metaphor for what has
happened in 1917; the "roof", or the logic of human
existence has disappeared and the reality of life,
like walls built of "clay and straw," is crumbling
into anarchy. In the midst of this, Shklovsky tries
to construct a framework which will make sense of
these events for him; the metaphor for this process is
the rooftop and the framework is the personal history
which he is writing. This connection is made clear in
an earlier passage where Shklovsky describes his arrival in Tabriz from Moscow, and his discovery of how
much in disarray things had fallen:

> That's how it was-- the houses had
> lost their roofs, the people had
> somewhat lost their heads, but they
> had long since grown accustomed to
> this state of affairs. (75)

Shklovsky implies the connection between roofs and
rationality by juxtaposing the houses and the people
in this passage, a technique he uses throughout the
novel. And farther on, to describe what happened to
a city near Tabriz after his arrival:

> It was plundered right up to the
> roofs, that is, completely leveled;
> although no one plunders clay walls,
> without roofs they dissolve in the
> rain and only the baseboards remain.
> The roofs were removed and sold. (95)

Shklovsky's point is that through corruption and hard-
ship, the "roof of the time" had been removed or sold,
and no amount of reason and logic could make sense of
this period. "Revolution and the Front" is the record
of Shklovsky's attempt to make sense of the events
around him, having been "driven . . . to the brink, as
the moon draws a somnambulist to the roof."(74)[17] The
cruelty and despair Shklovsky finds whirling about him
is incomprehensible to him in conventional terms, and
so he must find a "roof" of his own from which to
understand these experiences. Early in the novel
Shklovsky outlined his difficulties with this idea to
the reader:

> Writing about war is very difficult.
> Of all that I've read, the only thing
> I can remember as a plausible descrip-
> tion of it are Stendhal's Waterloo and
> Tolstoy's battle scenes. To describe
> the mood of a front without resorting
> to false and artificial passages is
> just as hard. Never -- not even while
> landing -- would any aviator be able
> to hear words -- even the most touching
> ones. Anyone who has flown at all knows
> it's impossible. Until I'm shown the
> statistics, I will never believe that
> there was so much fighting with bayonets
> on the western front or that it was
> possible to destroy a German foxhole
> with your hands and cave in the hole
> with your feet. I will never believe
> in this book, with its jumble of
> corpses, its end washed away by a
> flood and various conclusions. (59)

Shklovsky's point is clear: it is impossible to understand history, or any significant event from a conventional, objective point of view which yields only
"false and artificial passages." A personal, subjective history must take its place (the memoir) and this
is what Shklovsky apparently comes to terms with in
Part Two, "Writing Desk," where he parodies Part One
(which is still more closely related to the memoir),
and so paves the way for the nonfiction novel.18

"Writing Desk" begins with the motif of the
Falling Stone which has now replaced the roof image
as the major motif of the novel:

> When you fall like a stone, you don't
> need to think; when you think, you
> don't need to fall. I confused two
> occupations. The forces moving me
> were external to me. The forces moving
> others were external to them. I am
> only a falling stone. A stone that
> falls and can, at the same time, light
> a lantern to observe its own course. (133)

Here, Shklovsky seems to have accommodated his turbulent situation, and clarified for himself his own role
in these events. As a falling stone, Shklovsky and
those with him have no sense that they control their

35

destinies; they are like falling stones upon which "external forces" operate.[19] Shklovsky describes his own role as a "stone that falls and can, at the same time, light a lantern to observe his own course." It is clear from this that Shklovsky is writing a personal history ("his own course") and not a memoir or novel which would try to be applicable to la condition humaine.[20] In two other passages, Shklovsky refers to himself as a falling stone:

> But I am an art theoretician. I am a falling stone and, looking down, I know what motivation is! (179)

and

> I am a falling stone - professor of Art History, founder of the Russian school of the formal method (or morphological). In this situation I'm like a needle without any thread, passing through the cloth and leaving no trace. (226)

In both instances, it is important that Shklovsky mentions his artistic work and affiliation because in "Writing Desk" he parodies much of his work and many of the assumptions mentioned in "Revolution and the Front."

"Writing Desk" is far more disjointed and loosely constructed than Part One, and Shklovsky seems concerned here not only with characterizing the time and events for the reader, but also with disrupting the reader's expectations for this kind of text. The two major aesthetic points he emphasizes are the question of his own credibility as recorder of these events and, in connection with this, the problem of invention in a "documentary" recording of this kind. Shklovsky alludes to the tension between the individual experience and the fictional account which threatens his own individuality; this tension becomes the strongest unifying element in the narrative of A Sentimental Journey. Shortly after "Writing Desk" begins, Shklovsky describes a man who has been sent to him named Semyonov as "somehow not real," and then abruptly addresses the reader:

> I don't know whether this is compre-

> hensible. If it isn't, go talk to
> Semyonov yourself. He won't turn
> your stomach. (134)

A few pages later, Shklovsky again turns from the
narrative to the reader and suddenly, without either
preparatory or explanatory material, chides the reader
for his (assumed) disbelief:

> If you don't believe that there was a
> revolution, go and put your hand in
> the wound. It's wide. The hole was
> pierced by a three inch shell. (142)

Aside from implicitly comparing Russia to Christ,
Shklovsky also disrupts the expectations of his reader
and directs the reader's attention to the fact that
this is not an objective history but a _personal_ one;
it is more than a mere compilation and arrangement of
historical data.21 The suggestion here is that
Shklovsky selected and arranged, perhaps even changed
or partly invented the material, in order to best
convey his sense of "truth" about the situation he
lived through. Many of the direct references in the
novel ask the reader to be aware and critical, to be
more cognizant of his role in the writing process
than, for example, the "automatic" reader of conventional prose.

In addition to playing with the reader's expectations concerning his credibility as narrator, Shklovsky also casts doubt on the veracity of the stories
and anecdotes he presents to the reader as "history."
In the beginning of "Writing Desk," Shklovsky tells
the story about a peaceful demonstration in Petersburg
which has been dispersed, and about how the store-
keeper had made broom handles out of the placards:

> The yardkeepers later made broom
> handles out of the sticks from the
> placard. All this happened without
> me and I'm writing about it from
> other people's words. But I did
> see the broom handles-the very ones
> made from the placard. (135)

Shklovsky's point here, it seems, is not to make the
reader suddenly suspect that everything in A Sentimental Journey is invented, but rather to help the reader

see and understand that history is recorded through
the eyes of one perspective, in this case of Viktor
Shklovsky, who selects, arranges, and relates information as it best serves his understanding of things.
This is necessary because, along with the reader,
Shklovsky cannot know other perspectives; he can only
assume them as "poses", and thus fictionalize or
invent them as they might have happened. The only
valid and credible point of view to him is his own.
This very issue Shklovsky realizes in part one, and
he warns himself against "resorting to false and
artificial passages." This he tries to do straight-
forwardly, but unsuccessfully in "Revolution and the
Front." But his determination to "try to relate how
I understand everything that happened"(59) finally
means that he must move away from convention toward
nonfiction, because the typical, omniscient narrative
of the conventional form would require his adopting
an objective, "God-like" perspective which he cannot
know. This same point is made toward the end of the
text when Shklovsky "discovers" a manuscript written
by Lazar Zervandov, a wartime acquaintance who was
with him in Persia and remained to fight with the
Aissor detachment after the Russian detachment left.
Before relating the manuscript <u>in toto</u> to the reader,
Shklovsky inserts the following:

> Here's the manuscript of Lazar
> Zervandov himself. All I did was
> rearrange the punctuation and cor-
> rect the cases a little. Conse-
> quently, it's come out sounding
> like me.(259)

When the reader discovers that the "manuscript" contains information almost identical to an account
Shklovsky presented earlier, his (Shklovsky's) motive
becomes clear. Everything in this text is arranged
and filtered through the consciousness of Viktor
Shklovsky and will serve his own personal, subjective
design for how the text should best present the
"truth." This difference between "truth" in an objective sense--as in the conventional historical
memoir--and "truth" in the subjective, personal sense
which Shklovsky establishes in "Writing Desk" is implied in this ironic passage:

> And here I've put together the pieces
> of an absolutely true story--how Kherson

> was defended against the Germans.
> In general, everything I write in
> this book is the truth. None of
> the names have been changed.(221)

By this time, the aware reader understands that simply
using nonfictitious names does not ensure that the
"truth" is being told.

The device in which a story is told to a narrator
who in turn tells the same to the reader is simply
another variation of the "discovered manuscript" device, and is a common device in the conventional
memoir.22 Thus, Shklovsky parodies this technique in
"Writing Desk," as well as "bares" it, making the
reader aware that the "discovered manuscript" is in
fact a device:

> In other words, halfway through the
> novel, the action moves back in time
> by one of three devices: the reading
> of a "discovered manuscript," a dream
> of reminiscences of the hero .... the
> purpose of this device is retardation.
> The motivation... is a story, a manu-
> script, reminiscence, a mistake by
> the bookbinder (Immermann), the
> forgetfulness of the author (Sterne,
> Pushkin) or a cat's coming along and
> mixing the pages (Hoffman). (233)

By pointing out the literaturnost, the "literariness"
of the entire narrative, Shklovsky clearly parodies
the conventional form. Part of the overall intention
of A Sentimental Journey, aside from making sense of
history for Shklovsky, seems to be to parody the
convention and thus to initiate movement toward a new
genre, which we recognize as the nonfiction novel.

When Shklovsky published A Sentimental Journey in
1923, his Formalist colleagues Boris Eichenbaum and
Yury Tynyanov welcomed it as "the start of a promising
new trend in the novel," which "had been in a state
of crisis since the deaths of Dostoevsky, Turgenev,
and Tolstoy."23 More important, the "subject matter
and techniques of those masters no longer suited the
post revolutionary era. The genre required total
renewal."24 Thus, both the conventional realistic
novel and the conventional memoir forms (used in Russia

by Dostoevsky, Tolstoy, Aksakov, and Gorky)[25] were
indeed inadequate to express the "truth" perceived by
the artists of Soviet Russia's early turbulent, war-
torn years. And, A Sentimental Journey is by our
definition clearly a nonfiction novel: the first person narrative--which identifies Shklovsky as the
narrator, character and recorder--relates events and
occurrences which are factual along with dates, per-
sons, and political developments which are the narrative. Shklovsky relates personal and biographical
information through his personal geneology (page 226)
and his affiliation with Opoyaz, the Formalist group
(page 216), as well as in the intimate details of his
nightmares (page 163) and the deaths of his brothers
(pages 147, 156). The narrative emphasizes that it
presents a subjective view of reality, as opposed to a
shared, common reality which Shklovsky considers impossible. Finally, A Sentimental Journey contains,
"in addition to the story of its own composition, its
own esthetic";[26] in other words, the novel has a
strong metafictional dimension. Thus, we can agree
with Sidney Monas that one "might call A Sentimental
Journey . . . a kind of 'nonfiction novel' . . .."[27]
It is fitting, somehow, that Shklovsky's nonfiction
memoir which is named after the memoir of his most
influential predecessor, Lawrence Sterne, should in
turn become a parody (in part) of that form, just as
Stern's major novel, Tristran Shandy ("the most
typical novel"), is a parody of the Richardsonian
sentimental novel convention. Thus, the first nonfiction novel of the Twentieth Century was not American
but Russian.

NOTES

[1]Ultimately more so than Shklovsky's theoretical work with the Russian Formalists for the purposes of this study.

[2]This is partly due, we can assume, to the fact that some time elapsed between the writing of Parts One and Two (from May 1919 to May 1920), during which time Shklovsky's civil difficulties with the new Russian Government occurred.

[3]Richard Sheldon, Introduction to <u>A Sentimental Journey</u>, by Viktor Shklovsky, trans. by Richard Sheldon (Ithaca: Cornell University Press, 1970), p. xii.

[4]"When Shklovsky wrote Part One in 1919, he had not yet wholly evolved his distinctive Sternian manner yet. His primary aim was to provide an objective chronicle of the events in which he participated." Ibid., p. xviii.

[5]Ibid., p. xii.

[6]Viktor Shklovsky, "Art as Technique," in <u>Russian Formalist Criticism: Four Essays</u>, trans. and ed. by Lee T. Lemon and Marion J. Reis (Lincoln, Neb.: University of Nebraska Press, 1965), p. 12. Since this discussion is by no means an exhaustive or complete review of Shklovsky's work, the reader is directed especially to Richard Sheldon, "Viktor Borisovič Shklovsky: Literary Theory and Practice, 1914-1930." (Unpublished Dissertation, University of Michigan, 1966), and Victor Erlich, <u>Russian Formalism: History and Decline</u> (The Hague: Mouton & Company, 1965).

[7]cf. Robert H. Stacy, <u>Defamiliarization in Language and Literature</u> (New York: Syracuse University Press, 1977), Ch. 1.

[8]As Shklovsky's later work on the cinema attests, his theory seems true of any rhetorical discourse, from cinema to drama to even minute and significant personal acts between 2 people which can in fact be-

come meaningless ritual if each is repeated in an identical manner without changes in form or context.

[9] cf. James Kinneavy, <u>A Theory of Discourse</u> (New Jersey: Prentice-Hall, Inc. 1971), pp. 307-337.

[10] Erlich, p. 194, see also Zavarzadeh, p. 37.

[11] This is also discussed usefully in Frederic Jameson, <u>The Prison-House of Language</u> (Princeton: Princeton University Press, 1972), pp. 52-54.

[12] Viktor Shklovsky, <u>O teorii prozy</u> (Moscow, 1929), p. 227, as quoted in Jameson, p. 53.

[13] Viktor Shklovsky, <u>A Sentimental Journey</u>, trans. by Richard Sheldon (Ithaca, New York: Cornell University Press, 1970), p. 233. All subsequent references will be taken from this edition. See also the introductory essay in Victor E. Neuburg, <u>Popular Literature: A History and Guide</u> (MIddlesex, UK: Penquin Books, Ltd., 1977).

[14] "<u>Tristram Shandy</u> is the most typical novel in World Literature," in Viktor Shklovsky, "Sterne's <u>Tristram Shandy</u>: Stylistic Commentary," in <u>Russian Formalist Criticism: Four Essays</u>, trans. and ed. by Lee T. Lemon and Marion J. Reis (Lincoln, Neb.: University of Nebraska Press, 1965), p. 57.

[15] i.e., "Sterne's <u>Tristram Shandy</u>: Stylistic Commentary."

[16] "I don't like Barbusse's book <u>Under Fire</u>--it's glossy and contrived.", Shklovsky, <u>A Sentimental Journey</u>, p. 59.

[17] The same is true of Norman Mailer's writing situation with <u>The Armies of The Night</u> and the Vietnam War protest of 1968.

[18] Again, this closely parallels the situation--especially the relationship of the two parts of the novel--with Mailer's <u>The Armies of The Night</u>.

[19]Already this is quite a change from the Nineteenth Century convention, where man's control over his own destiny was simply assumed.

[20]Almost certainly, the allusion here is to Euripides' play <u>Heracles</u>, in which both the image of the falling roof as a collapse of reason ["He slumped to the floor and hit his back against a pillar which had fallen there, snapped in two pieces when the roof collapsed.(345)"] and the image of the falling stone ["Oh to be a stone! to feel no grief!(362)"] are used to describe Heracles' horror at the cruelty perpetrated through him on his family by Hera. cf. Euripides, "Heracles" in <u>Euripides I</u>, ed. by David Greene and Richmond Lattimore (New York: Random House, 1956).

[21]By implication, Shklovsky--as well as the other nonfiction writers--suggests that even "objective" and nonpersonal histories are in fact not so, having been compiled and arranged by some <u>one</u> who has interests and feelings which will affect the selection process.

[22]Shklovsky also uses it in "Revolution and the Front," for example on p. 99.

[23]Sheldon, Introduction to <u>A Sentimental Journey</u>, p. xv.

[24]Ibid.

[25]Sidney Monas, "Driving Nails With a Samovar: A Historical Introduction" in <u>A Sentimental Journey</u>, trans. by Richard Sheldon (Ithaca: Cornell University Press, 1970), p. xxix.

[26]Ibid.

[27]Ibid.

CHAPTER THREE:

JAMES AGEE AND LET US NOW PRAISE FAMOUS MEN

> Ausdrücklich 'Phantasie' heißt der erste Satz,
> der zweite ist ein in mächtiger steigerung sich
> erhebendes Adagio, der dritte ein Finale, das leicht,
> fast spielerisch einsetzt, sich kontrapunktisch
> zunehmend verdichtet und zugleich immer mehr den
> Charakter tragischen Ernstes annimmt, bis es in einem
> dusteren, trauermarschähnlichen Epilog sich endigt.
> . . . 'Ich habe,' sagte Adrian zu mir, 'keine Sonate
> schreiben wollen, sondern einen Roman.'   Thomas Mann

*   *   *

Like Viktor Shklovsky thirteen years earlier,
James Agee wrote Let Us Now Praise Famous Men during a
period of trauma, both for him personally, and socially
and politically in the United States. The Nineteen
Thirties were for the United States perhaps the most
difficult and troubling years prior to the Vietnam War
protest decade of the Nineteen Sixties. These were
the years of the Great Depression and, partly as a
consequence, the period when the American Left gained
the most political ground and appealed to the greatest
number of people.[1] Many of the same value upheavals
which occurred in Russia over a decade prior occurred
in the U.S. between 1930 and 1938, and fostered a
period of intellectual tolerance during which a number
of artists experimented with new forms and styles.[2]
In 1932, James Agee graduated from Harvard University,
already a published poet, and within one month, signed
as a writer with the business journal Fortune, "dedicated by the Founder [Henry Luce] to American Business,
considered as the heart of the American Scene."[3]
Although he had established strong ties with the American Left, Agee joined staff writers Dwight MacDonald[4]
and Archibald MacLeish (who would later edit Agee's
first book of poetry, Permit Me Voyage), and together
they fostered at Fortune a more critical attitude
towards American capitalism. From the beginning, Agee
was dissatisfied with his job, which usually consisted
of researching and writing arcane articles on the
benefits of American capitalism, and he sought to
leave the U.S. for Europe to concentrate on writing

poetry, especially to work on his long poem entitled
<u>John Carter</u>. Early in 1933, Agee applied unsuccess-
fully (the first of two unsuccessful attempts) for a
Guggenheim Fellowship to France, and one of the projects he suggested in the application was an experiment with poetic diction and imagery in the short
story form, tentatively called "Let Us Now Praise
Famous Men."[5] The story was inspired by the passage
in Ecclesiastes,[6] and no doubt bore some resemblance
to his later work of the same name.

During this period, the major trends in American
writing were the "proletarian novel," practiced by
Micheal Gold, Henry Roth, and Jack Conroy, and "documentary reportage" dominated by Margaret Bourke-White,
Russell Lee, and Dorothea Lange.[7] The "proletarian
novel," especially the novels of Micheal Gold,
exhibited the major characteristics of the conventional
realistic novel with the "plight of the worker" as its
major subject focus.[8] In fact, the American proletarian novel, like the novels of Socialist Realism in the
Soviet Union, had become almost formulaic, and too
often, the literary qualities of the novel were sacri-
ficed to the political "ritualization" of party and
class.[9] Thus, little had changed in the realistic
novel since the previous century, except perhaps in
the didactic, nearly propagandistic tone of some of
the less subtle examples.[10] While the conventional
novel <u>assumed</u> a shared reality, the proletarian novel
<u>insisted</u> that the realities of the worker's world
were the only legitimate subject. More significant,
however, was the documentary genre which eventually
dominated much of the popular writing of the 1930's.
The increased exposure and popular agitation of the
American Left provided the public with a conscience,
and increasingly more space in journals and studies
was devoted to documenting America's social ills. In
his excellent work on documentary expression, William
Stott characterized the role of the writer in documentary writing thus:

> In . . . documentary writing . . .
> confession was a strategy for tele-
> graphing to the audience the feelings
> it should feel. The writer was an
> experiencer of a certain social condi-
> tion, and his firsthand reactions were
> to guide the reader's own. The writer's
> personality figured in the report, if at

all, in abbreviated form, as a type:
usually the cool-headed fact-gatherer
or the weeping Jeremiah. His complexities and passions, and the full story
of how he got the story were left out
of account.[11]

So, in terms of narrative assumption and point of view,
the documentary was not very different from the realistic novel. In both forms, an omniscient narrator
described a shareable view of the world across an
aesthetic distance which precluded describing his own
"complexities and passions" in the text, even though
these had profoundly affected the text-narrative. The
journalist or the documentor assumed a role ("type")
in the text (usually omniscient) and recorded a part
of the real world which he shared with the reader:
one, moreover, which the reader had been reluctant to
acknowledge up to this point. Since the recorder
wrote about and photographed a world which was equally
his and the reader's, then he (the recorder) could
well "guide the reader's own" reaction to the material,
thus eliciting an "approved" response to the text.
The most typical documentary of this type is Margaret
Bourke-White's You Have Seen Their Faces (New York,
1937), part of which Agee used in an article on the
Great Drought.[12] As Stott shows in his discussion of
the documentary, this and other documentary texts
sought to emphasize the pathetic and degrading existence of the southern and midwestern poor in order to
elicit pity in the reader.[13]

This sort of writing was current when in 1936,
Fortune assigned Agee to do a documentary report on
the Southern white sharecropping farmer:

[to] do a story on: A Sharecropper
family (daily and yearly life): and
also a study of Farm Economics in
the South . . .: and also on the
several efforts to help the situation: i.e., Government and State
work; theories and wishes of
Southern liberals. . ..[14]

Agee, when asked whom he would like to accompany him
as photographer, immediately requested and got Walker
Evans of the Farm Services Administration of the U.S.
Department of Agriculture.[15] Because of a previous

research trip (1935) he made to Tennessee while
working on an article concerning the Tennessee Valley
Authority and its incursion into the lives of poor
farmers, Agee originally planned to spend one month in
Tennessee working on his new assignment for Fortune.
By June, 1936, the two men had decided to go to Alabama, where they spent slightly over eight weeks
working on what eventually became Let Us Now Praise
Famous Men.

Let Us Now Praise Famous Men was not developed
according to a critical theory such as Shklovsky's
theory of ostranenie, nor is it structured neatly
into text and parody as is A Sentimental Journey. In
a real sense, Agee did not have the same distance from
his text, and so conscious parody does not occur as
frequently as in A Sentimental Journey. Even so,
Agee's novel is as innovative within the American
novel tradition as Shklovsky's novel is within the
Russian prose tradition. Thematically, the novel
follows two distinguishable lines of development. The
first is the most subjective since it traces Agee's
gradual coming to terms with his ambivalent feelings
about himself, about his work, and about the sharecroppers. The second thematic line is a metafictional
one, and reflects Agee's attempts to separate Let Us
Now Praise Famous Men from both the conventional
realistic novel and from the documentary form; this
plane eventually produces an implicit description of
the nonfiction novel. Both thematic levels are often
fused together, and much of what Agee tries to resolve
in terms of his work, for example, eventually reveals
information which is important for his description of
the nonfiction novel. This is especially true in the
middle section, "On the Porch: 2." Structurally, the
novel is arranged vertically rather than horizontally
(Or in a linear fashion), as would be the case in a
conventional, "totalizing" narrative. It might be
said that the plot of Let Us Now Praise Famous Men is
completely subjective, personal, and internal: few of
the sections coincide chronologically, and very little
concrete and temporal information concerning the time
when Agee is actually writing is provided, except in
the section "Intermission: Conversation in the Lobby,"
and in two footnotes on page 357, a full three-quarters
into the novel. Rather, the text traces Agee's gradual recognition of the intensity of his experience
with the sharecroppers, his subsequent struggle to
work within conventional forms and eventual description

of the nonfiction novel, and finally, we sense his
change in values from the beginning of the period he
spent in Alabama to the point when he is ready to
return to New York. In this sense, the text is an
intense and self-reflexive künstlerroman, and the
narrative moves from occasion to occasion, object to
object as they occur to Agee in his transcription of
these important changes within himself. Thus, the
plot progresses associatively and vertically, almost
at random, to the center of the novel and "On the
Porch: 2." which is the "highest" narrative and emotional point in the text.

There are three "On the Porch" sections, and each
marks a distinct point in the development of the narrative. "On the Porch: 1" is the ostensible beginning
of the novel, but is stopped short while Agee side-
steps to another more personal section which helps the
reader understand the emotional change recorded by the
novel. James Agee, the reader suspects, is not yet
able (personally and as a writer) to convey the intense
and powerful experience in the novel, partially because he has not yet described the parameters of the
nonfiction novel form. "On the Porch: 2" is the most
important and most intense section of the novel,
because here the personal and metafictional planes of
the text are fused completely; each time Agee moves
beyond a difficult point in his own psychological
development the text supplies a metafictional passage
which separates his work from both the conventional
realistic novel and the documentary form. The third
and final "On the Porch" section occurs at the end of
the novel, and is closest in tone to the first "On the
Porch" section, since Agee is now prepared emotionally
and artistically to continue the text he began in that
first section. Thus, Let Us Now Praise Famous Men is
structured vertically instead of in a conventional
linear form, and the plot, correspondingly, is extremely subjective, and proceeds in a cyclical,
associative manner between the three "On the Porch"
sections.

It would be difficult to find a more "literary,"
or artistically contrived text. Let Us Now Praise
Famous Men is also clearly not an example of journalism,
or of documentary, for, in addition to Agee's remarks
concerning these forms in the text, no journal, magazine, or documentary series would accept such a
hermetic, intensely personal work for public distribu-

49

tion. Fortune's rejection of Agee's manuscript upon
his return to New York underlines this point; the
formal category within which Let Us Now Praise Famous
Men can best be defined is the nonfiction novel,[16]
primarily because the material recorded within the
text is private, not shared. This point explains in
part the critical confusion which Agee's novel created
when it was finally published, and then only upon the
strong recommendation of a personal friend of his.[17]
Finally, to understand Let Us Now Praise Famous Men as
a nonfiction novel, the relationships between each
section of the text must be explored, especially the
"On the Porch" chapters. Agee's rapid and troubling
shifts from "On the Porch: 1" to "On the Porch: 3"
reveal the reasons for his adoption of the nonfiction
form.

The novel proper begins on page nineteen of Book
Two; Book One contains very little material which
specifically concerns the tenant farmers or Agee's
experience with them. Before this come Walker Evan's
photographs--the first thirty-three pages of the book-
-then a title page, followed by a Preface and other
short verses and texts (mostly quoted) which are
surely meant to confuse and antagonize the reader.
Evan's photographs comprise a text almost by themselves,[18] and are a marked contrast to the melodramatic, exaggerated, and pathetic photographs in the
documentaries of Margaret Bourke-White. For example,
they record the simple elegance and beauty of poor
sharecropping families posing to have their pictures
taken:[19]

> Evan does not "expose" the reality
> he treats, he reveals it--or better,
> he lets it reveal itself. He does
> not seek out [as M. Bourke-White
> does], he in fact avoids, the spec-
> tacular, the odd, the piteous, the
> unseemly.[20]

To avoid the superfluous, no commentary, title, or
explanatory material accompanies the photos; the
portraits stand by themselves. Following the title
page, a two-part "Preface" describes the circumstances
of Agee's and Evan's trip to Alabama (Part One), and
then describes the intention and design of the text
(Part Two). Part one is narrated by both Agee and
Evans; Part Two is Agee's alone. Serious readers,

Agee suggests, "are advised to proceed [beyond Part Two] after finishing the first section of the Preface," since "a later return will do no harm." (xiii) This comment is perhaps the most conscious example of parody in the novel.

In the second part of the Preface, Agee describes his subject, his role as recorder, and the manner in which the text ought to be read. Nominally, the subject is "North American cotton tenantry examined in the daily living of three representative tenant families." Actually, however, "the effort is to recognize the stature of a portion of unimagined existence, and to contrive techniques proper to its recording, communication, analysis, and defense. (xiv) [Italics added]" Thus, from the start, we learn of Agee's need for a different literary form through which to communicate his experience, and he explicitly makes this search for a new form part of the design of the text. Thus, the internal mechanism of the novel lies in the movement from the plane of Agee's personal experience to the more objective metafictional narrative plane where the subject focus includes Agee, the tenants, and the text:

> The immediate instruments [in recording] are two: the motionless camera, and the printed word. The governing instrument--which is also one of the centers of the subject-- is individual, anti-authoritative human consciousness. [italics added] (xiv)

Agee also suggests in the Preface that Let Us Now Praise Famous Men be read aloud, because "variations of tone, pace, shape, and dynamics are here particularly unavailable to the eye alone, and with their loss, a good deal of meaning escapes. (xv)" The text should also be read continuously, "as music is listened to or a film watched" (xv) in order to ensure an aesthetic organicity similar to that from which it was created. Finally, Agee warns, this "is a book only by necessity; . . . a piece of the body torn out by the roots might be more to the point." (xvi, 13) Thus the Preface provides clues to the reader in to what he can expect of the novel proper: the narrative will not be a documentary narrated by a "cool-headed fact-gatherer" or a "weeping Jeremiah," but, will record Agee's personal and aesthetic experience with three tenant families in Alabama.

After the Preface, the text is divided into Books One and Two; Book One, only five pages long (including two pages listing all the "characters"), consists of "Preliminaries" or quotations from other texts which are placed there probably to confuse and mislead the "conventional" reader.[21] Crucial to Agee's distinction between the conventional novel and the nonfiction novel is the fact that the reader of conventional fiction reads "automatically;" this is one point he wishes to change. Book Two begins the novel proper and records Agee's and Evans's work in Southern Alabama.[22] In this "core" of the novel, Agee tries to reproduce his multifaceted experience of the tenants' lives as a simultaneous whole, but the inability of "normal" language to convey more than one dimension of this material forces him to present only one level at a time. In this instance, language fails the writer, and another form will be required to recreate Agee's experience. Thus the narrative occasionally shifts from the most specific and minute aspect of these people's lives to a perspective which for a moment suspends several different levels of existence and experience. Aside from Agee's intent, these narrative shifts also demonstrate the literaturnost, the "literariness" of the novel.

In a "Preamble" inserted between a short poem dedicated to Walker Evans and the first "on the Porch" section, Agee defines his role in the text, as well as the unusual nature of this particular novel. To begin, Agee claims that for a commercial journal like Fortune to hire him and Evans to intrude into the lives of these simple people in the name of "journalism" is "curious, obscene, terrifying, and unfathomably mysterious.(8)" [23] After this, he addresses the reader:

> [The] question, Who are you will
> read these words and study these
> photographs, and through what
> cause, by what chance, and for
> what purpose, and by what right do
> you qualify to, and what will you
> do about it; and the question, Why
> we make this book, and set it as
> large, and by what right, and for

> what purpose, and to what good end,
> or none . . .. (9)

Thus, the reader is never taken lightly in the novel, and as Robert Fitzgerald notes, Agee understood that what is "the case [in <u>Let Us Now Praise Famous Men</u>] in some degree proceeded from the observer."[24] Agee also insists that his reader be critical and aware, in order that he experience the material in the text as intensely as Agee had.[25] Also in the Preamble, Agee suggests that the conventional novel, to use Shklovsky's terms, has become "automatic" and is inadequate to convey his own emotional involvement within the text:

> In a [conventional realistic] novel,
> a house or a person has his meaning,
> his existence entirely through the
> writer. Here, a house or a person
> has only the most limited of his
> meaning through me: his true meaning
> is much larger. It is that he exists,
> in actual being [and is not a type],
> as you and as I do, and as no charac-
> ter of the imagination can possibly
> exist. (12)

Thus Agee insists that unlike the conventional realistic novel, neither the characters nor the narrator (who is Agee) in this novel are fictional; they are also not manipulated to serve a private interpretation, as they would be in the documentary.[26] To prevent the reader from reading the text in this conventional manner, Agee insists that he abandon the traditional, "totalizing" conception of art: "in God's name don't think of it [the text] as art." (15)

In effect, the Preamble is identical to the second half of the Preface, which Agee had suggested the "serious reader" avoid reading. The "serious reader" is the one whose reading expectations Agee wishes to violate and change. Thus, Agee explicitly contradicts the stated intention of his Preface, mostly to disrupt and (as with Shklovsky) prolong the reader's conventional "retraining" as a reader. Told not to read the second half of the Preface, the reader will do precisely the opposite. However, nearly the same material occurs some ten pages later, and the reader's attention will likely shift from what he

53

expects will follow in the narrative to consider how Agee has violated these expectations and, more importantly, why he has violated them. The reader is then "forced" to become more critical; he must consider the writing process a part of the subject matter in the text. The reader of Let Us Now Praise Famous Men becomes the "would-be-novelist."

After these preliminary sections, the text proper of Let Us Now Praise Famous Men begins. The novel is structured in five parts--similar perhaps to a five act Shakespearean tragedy[27] or, as critic Peter Ohlin suggests, according to the "careful symmetry" of a Beethoven symphony. [28] There are three major descriptive sections: "Part One, A country Letter," "Part Two: Some Findings and Comments," and "Part Three: Inductions." These sections are "framed" by the three "On the Porch" sections, which contain Agee's personal, sometimes angrily defensive ruminations about his work and the tenant farmers. "Part Two: Some Findings and Comments: is divided by "On the Porch 2"--which is placed at the exact physical and thematic center of the text--and this bifurcated Part Two is then separated from Parts One and Three by secondary sections entitled "Colon" and "Intermission: Conversation in the Lobby."

As a result of this cyclical and ascending structure, Let Us Now Praise Famous Men has greater thematic unity when explained from the middle outward than from either the first or the last pages inward. "On the Porch: 2" is the thematic, structural and emotional core of the novel in addition to its literal center. Thus, the most "objective" documentary information is contained in Part Two, where Agee describes in detail the tenant farmer's shelter (123-221), money (115-122), clothing articles (255-286), education (287-316), and finally, his work (317-347), with which Agee is most sympathetic, since work in this case defines both the existences of the tenants and Agee's existence.[29] These shorter sections mostly describe objects (including the now famous description of the Gudger bureau in their front bedroom, p. 161), and mention the tenants only if knowledge of their daily existence would help the reader understand the significance of these objects (for example, the discussion of types of shoes, worn differently from husband to wife, in the clothing section, pp. 262-263). Towards the end of each section, Agee draws certain parallels between the three tenant families and, occasionally, between them and the "outside" world of which Agee and the reader are aware, while the tenants are not. This sense of existential simultaneity, which indicates the points of greatest intensity for Agee, is strongest and most sustained in the section on shelter. Agee arrives at this particular simultaneity through association from a listing of vegetables found in the Gudger garden and he sustains it for over a page and a half, ending with:

> and they are all drawn into the one
> and hottest room, the parents; the
> children; and beneath the table the
> dog and the puppy and the sliding
> cats, and above it, a grizzling
> literal darkness of flies, and spread
> on all quarters, the simmering dream
> held in this horizon yet overflowing
> it, and of the natural world, and
> eighty miles back east and north, the
> hard flat incurable sore of Birming-
> ham. (219-220)

And, at the end of this introspective, intensely subjective section comes "On the Porch: 2". As mentioned earlier, these layers of simultaneous existence not only reflect Agee's aesthetic and experiential process, but also mirror the reading process. The extemporaneous material he includes in the novel clarifies his own personality (for us and for him) as he experiences the tenants. The reader repeats this process as he reads the novel, since neither Agee nor the reader is a "passive information-processing instrument."[30]

"On the Porch: 1", which started the novel, is clearly the beginning of the text Agee will eventually write, after "On the Porch: 2." However, he cuts this beginning short (after less than three pages) because he must first distinguish his text from existing conventional forms. As we mentioned in chapter one, this is typical of a self-conscious text; the artist's personality and existence are as important within the narrative as either the subject matter or the process of recording the text. The novel argues for the validity of Agee's personal experience as well as for its own aesthetic validity and integrity. And so, "On the Porch: 1" begins with a description of the

Gudger home where, we later learn, Agee lived during most of his stay in Alabama. His description reflects both his impression of the Gudgers and his individual personality as he begins to speak:

> The house and all that was in it had
> now descended deep beneath the gradual
> spiral it had sunk through; it lay
> formal under the order of entire silence.
> In the square pine room at the back the
> bodies of the man of thirty [George
> Gudger] and of his wife and of their
> children lay on shallow mattresses on
> their iron beds and on the rigid floor,
> and they were sleeping, and the dog lay
> asleep in the hallway. (19)

After moving to a room adjoining the Gudger bedroom, Agee writes as the exhausted Gudger family sleeps. He feels the intensity of his own consciousness as it touches the Gudger family, and just at the point when he is ready to begin the narrative, he ends the text abruptly on the words "We lay on the front porch:". The same phrase begins "On the Porch: 2" and only in "On the Porch: 3" does the line develop beyond this point both thematically and chronologically. But before, in "On the Porch: 2," Agee explores the new form he needs to continue. "On the Porch: 2," Agee tells the reader, was written

> to stand as the beginning of a much
> longer book, ... It is here
> intended still in part as a preface
> or opening, but also as a frame and
> as an undertone and as the set stage
> and center of action, in relation to
> which all other parts of this Volume
> are intended as flashbacks, foretastes,
> illuminations and contradictions. (245)

Thus, this second "On the Porch" section is the most significant in the novel, both for Agee's emotional/ phychological development and because it contains his description of the nonfiction novel.

Agee begins this section as he had the Preamble: by describing what he is <u>not</u> writing. Thus in this part of <u>Let Us Now Praise Famous Men</u>, Agee separates the realistic novel and the documentary (journalistic)

form from the nonfiction novel and defines the limits
of the nonfiction novel. He then explores his experiences with the sharecroppers, especially the Gudger
family, more fully and in greater depth than in any
other section of the novel. In "On the Porch: 2,"
Agee shifts from a third-person description to first-
person narration, a self conscious narrative mode,
and repeats: "We lay on the front porch." (223) Since
the book's "here is . . . human consciousness,"[31]
part of the aesthetic intensity Agee (and the reader)
perceives in the tenants' lives stems from their
simple, uncomplicated existence:

> We may do well to question whether
> there is anything more marvelous or
> more valuable in the state of being
> we distinguish as 'life' than in
> the state of being of a stone . . . .
> (226)[32]

This leads him to marvel, as he had in the beginning,
at the _fact_ of George Gudger's existence, as though
this fact suddenly affirmed his own presence in the
novel:

> It is that he [George Gudger] _exists_,
> in actual being, as you do and as I
> do, and as no character of the ima-
> gination can possibly exist. (12)
>
> The one deeply exciting thing to me
> about Gudger is that he is actual, he
> is living, at this instant. (240)

Agee often questions the legitimacy of his presence
and function in the novel, and the simple lives of
the Gudgers, the Woods, and the Ricketts as often seem
more significant and more enviable than his own
troubled life. Thus, Gudger's simple life affirms
Agee's tentative (in his own eyes) expression of it
within the pages of the text. For Agee, these people
have acquired meaning in their lives by asserting the
"symmetry" of their individual existences on the earth
they cultivate and inhabit: "[these people have] expressed themselves upon the grieved membrane of the
earth in the symmetry of a disease. . . ." (229) Agee
thus returns to his argument in the Preamble, and
characterizes his work in the novel as "an effort in
human actuality," bound up as much within his own life

as within the lives of the people he came to study.
For these tenants, hard subsistence work draws human
meaning from an asymmetrical, non-empirical universe.
And, within the context of <u>Let Us Now Praise Famous
Men</u>, one facet of this human assertion is the symmetry
of art, which Agee sees in the sharecropper's existence
(and they do not) and continually searches for in his
own.   This is one reason why the personal plane of
the narrative is so often fused with the more objective, metafictional narrative plane: the validity of
the tenants and their work confirms the validity of
his own work and his own life.

But here Agee is also caught in an impossible
paradox, which arises from his need to confront the
conventional realistic and documentary forms. His
intention is to "reproduce and communicate his [George
Gudger's] living as nearly exactly as possible . . .."
(233) This precludes any conscious invention, especially that which would probably occur if Agee
utilized an omniscient, conventional narrator. If he
did invent himself and these characters, the intensity
and accuracy he desired would be lost:

> I could invent incidents, appearances,
> additions to his George Gudger's
> character, background, surroundings,
> future, which might well point up and
> indicate and clinch things relevent
> to him which in fact I am sure are
> true, and important and which George
> Gudger unchanged and undecorated would
> not indicate and perhaps could not even
> suggest.[33] (233)

Agee would like the sharecroppers themselves to convey
the beauty and significance he sees in their lives,
free of embellishment. But at this point in the narrative, he concedes that this desire is "essentially
and finally a hopeless one" (233); in trying to remain
impartial and objective, he would become the "cool-
headed fact-gatherer" of the documentaries he depises.
The "objective" perspective of the journalist is, like
the omniscient point of view of the narrator in the
realistic novel, false and hypocritical, and does not
convey "artistic truth:"

> The very blood and semen of journalism
> . . . is a broad and successful form of

lying. Remove that form of lying
and you no longer have journalism.
(235)

Agee then distinguishes his work from the Nineteenth
Century realistic novel: "Nor am I speaking of
'naturalism,' 'realism'," conscious that within this
distinction "may be the sharpest and most slippery
watershed . . .." (235)[34] Thus, Agee correctly
perceives that the "falsifying" or "totalizing" process which he disavows in Let Us Now Praise Famous Men
is the same in both the documentary and the realistic
novel: a "reduction and depersonalization into terms
. . . of flat blank tremendously constructed chords
and of immensely elaborate counterpoint . . .." (235)
The author of Let Us Now Praise Famous Men places his
own personality as participant/observer between the
fictional devices of the novel and the reader, thus
creating the narrative tension crucial to nonfiction.
For Agee, the naturalistic novel is much closer to
documentary than it is to art: "that is why . . . [the
naturalist's] work even at best is never much more
than documentary." (237) [35] Let Us Now Praise Famous
Men proposes an alternative to these forms.

Objectivity within any text, Agee points out, is
impossible within the subjective structure of manmade
art.[36] Words do not fall together meaningfully outside of human consciousness and without human effort,
because language is the building substance invented
by man to convey and affirm value and order. It is
used to "assert a symmetry" upon a perceptual, phenomenological universe: "Words cannot embody; they can
only describe." (238) Thus, when an artist creates
characters and incidents from a traditional omniscient
perspective which implies that they have meaning or
significance outside the "perceiver", an unfortunate
illusion is perpetuated--one which is more deceptive
than the illusion created by art:

> [Art is] both nearer the truth and
> farther from it than those things
> which, like science and scientific
> art, merely describe, and those
> things which, like human beings and
> their creations and the entire
> state of nature, merely are, the
> truth. (238)

Agee concedes the artistic or contrived quality of <u>Let Us Now Praise Famous Men</u>, but only in that the text is arranged according to the specific perspective of James Agee. George Gudger is "not some artist's or journalist's or propagandist's invention" (240), but a man whom James Agee has experienced, and only <u>through</u> the record of this process will the reader ever know George Gudger:

> George Gudger is a man, et cetera. But, . . . in the effort to tell of him (by example) as truthfully as I can, I am limited. <u>I know him only so far as I know him, and only in those terms in which I know him; and all of that depends as fully on who I am as on who he is.</u> [italics added] (239)

This is the crucial aesthetic distinction which makes the nonfiction novel different. Agee cannot "know" these people; he can only know himself through them, and it is important for the reader to recognize James Agee in George Gudger and in all the other characters of the novel: "I would do just as badly to simplify or or eliminate myself from this picture as to simplify or invent character, places or atmospheres." (240) Thus his "voice" and personality stand clearly between the "fictional" text and the trained reader of fiction. In 1942, Agee wrote the introduction for a proposed book of photographs by Helen Levitt, an artist he admired, and in it is a statement which might serve as the aesthetic synthesis of his work on <u>Let Us Now Praise Famous Men</u>:

> The artist's task is not to alter the world as the eye sees it into a world of esthetic reality [as with the conventional forms], but to perceive the esthetic reality within the actual world, and to make an undisturbed and faithful record of the instant in which this movement of creativeness achieves its most expressive crystallization. [37]

Undoubtedly, in the more intense passages of the novel, Agee projects some of his own emotions into the situations and onto the people he describes. For example,

when George Gudger's sister-in-law Emma has to leave
the area to follow her new husband North, Agee recalls:

> Emma could spend her last few days
> . . . having a gigantic good time
> in bed, with George, a kind of a
> man she is best used to, and with
> Walker and with me, whom she is
> curious about and attracted to .
> . .. (62)

Then, speaking for Emma, George, Walker Evans and himself, he says that this idea "has a good many times in
the past couple of days come very clearly through
between all of us. . . ." (62) Nothing more is given
to support this observation, and the impression is
left intact with the reader. In fact, however, this
unself-conscious sexual attraction is probably solely
Agee's which he then projected upon Emma, George and
Walker Evans, who admitted some time later that he
found "the scene an embarrassment, since he is said
[by Agee] to have been harboring a disreputable idea
that in fact did not cross his mind."[38] But in spite
of Agee's embellishment, one can hardly accuse him of
lying or falsifying what actually occurred to change
the sense of the passage. He probably did feel sexually attracted to Emma, and was unable to keep his
emotion apart from his impression of the people around
him. But unlike the omniscient narrator of the realistic novel, Agee does not disguise his role in this
subjective process. There is no narrative "pose"
here. In fact, William Stott argues, Agee "verified
the tenant woman's reality as a human, a woman, and
not merely an integer in a criminal economy."[39] This
is, finally, Agee's point in Let Us Now Praise Famous
Men: to record for the reader his perception of the
tenant farmers' uncomplicated and beautiful lives.

Yet, by breaking away from the realistic novel
and the documentary, Agee also sees the danger that
the new, nonfiction form could also become convention,
and that the reader's participation in this literary
process would eventually become "automatic." The
uncritical and unaware reader of a conventional text
gets "so used to the idea that art is a fiction that
he can't shake himself of it." (241) One reason for
this concern is that Agee's own discrete personality
within Let Us Now Praise Famous Men would be threat-
ened with anonymity; as he states earlier: "I too

exist, not as a work of fiction, but as a human being."
(12) The conventional fiction reading process would
detract from the immediacy of Agee's prose, and com-
promise its unconventionality, its literaturnost--
which has confirmed Agee's and the tenants' lives in
the novel:

> Must it ["automatization," i.e.,
> deification] therefore interfere
> with still another way of seeing and
> telling of still another form of the
> truth which is in its own way at
> least as sound? (241-242)

Thus, Let Us Now Praise Famous Men is unconventional,
innovative art, and although Agee "may frequently try
to make use of art devices," (242) he creates a prose
form different from the existing forms. And his
dissatisfaction with both these conventional forms
and with the reader's usual way of reading partially
accounts for his occasional impatience with both the
task and the reader: "all I want to do is tell this
as exactly and clearly as I can and get the damned
thing done with." (243)

In the last ten pages of "On the Porch: 2", Agee
resumes his concrete description of the Gudger family.
He also characterizes the personal, narrative plane
which was strongest in this section:

> [The] "truest" thing about the ex-
> perience is now neither that it was
> from hour to hour thus and so; nor
> is it my fairly accurate "memory"
> of how it was from hour to hour in
> chronological progressions; but
> rather as it turns up in recall,
> in no such order, casting its lights
> and associations forward and back-
> ward upon the then past and the then
> future, across that expanse of
> experience. (244)

The reader can discern in this passage Agee's conten-
tion that recording the text means also re-experiencing
it. Moreover, reading the recorded text-narrative
results in a new and different impression for the
reader, which should still be as intense as Agee's
had been. Also, Agee explains, the narrative structure

is subjective and woven together out of four different kinds of experiential material. At the end of "On the Porch: 2", Agee "bares" the three part structure of the narrative for the reader:

> "As it happened": the straight
> narrative at the prow as from the
> first to last day it cut unknown
> water. By recall and memory from
> the present: which is a part of the
> experience: and this includes ima-
> gination, which in the other planes
> I swear myself against. As I try
> to write it: problems of recording;
> which, too, are an organic part of
> the experience as a whole. [italics
> added] (243)

This and his earlier discussions of the nature of art and its relationship to the individual writer prepare us for Agee's point that "nothing here is invented." (244)

Thus, in "On the Porch: 2", Agee reaches the thematic high point of the novel, both on the personal and metafictional narrative planes. It is important to recognize that Agee consciously works away from the conventional realistic novel (pages 12, 233, 235, 237, 240) as well as from the documentary (journalistic) convention (pages 235, 237, 240, 242). These metafic-tional remarks occur in the text at the same time as Agee describes a particularly intense personal occur-rance, and suggest that a.) the nonfiction novel form is better suited than the conventional realistic novel to convey a subjective experience, and b.) the non-fiction novel evolved from the traditional novel because the latter was no longer adequate to record these subjective, personal experiences.

Following the close of "On the Porch: 2", Part Two of Book Two, which comprises the longest section of the novel, ends with three short passages describ-ing the tenants' clothing, education, and work. Agee regains the broad narrative sweep of "On the Porch: 2" only in the section on education, wherein he chastizes pseudo-liberal, bourgeois interests (which Fortune magazine represents[40]) for having a.) neglected to give these tenant children even the rudiments of an elementary education which other American children enjoy, and b.) for having compounded this injury by presenting an "approved" lifestyle and value system in the children's books which they cannot understand, much less hope to enjoy.[41] Part Two is followed by a nine page section entitled "Intermission: Conversation In the Lobby," which consists of a questionnaire sent to Agee by the Partisan Review in May, 1939. The questionnaire, titled "Some Questions Which Face American Writers Today," consists of seven questions about America's "useable past"[42] and about the class structure of America's literary audience, in addition to inquiries about the writer's attitude toward American politics in the decade of the Nineteen Thirties and about the possibility of a European war. The questionnaire, along with his angry and irreverent responses (circa 1939), raises two different issues for the reader of Let Us Now Praise Famous Men. First, besides revealing Agee's connections with the American Left, the questionnaire provides more personal data about his life at the time when he wrote the novel. Secondly, Agee's public rejection of these activities also reflects his rejection of past conventions, both aesthetic and personal. Since he emerged from "On the Porch: 2" with many of his personal values changed, he must also have felt it necessary to reject the conventional aesthetic forms (the realistic novel and the documentary) which had stood in the way of the subjective, nonfiction novel he would write. "Intermission: Conversation in the Lobby" concludes this process.[43]

In "Part Three: Inductions," Agee returns to the lyrical narrative of "On the Porch: 2,"[44] but now he directly addresses the "co-celebrants" of his work: the tenants. The term "co-celebrants" is appropriate, since Part Three is loosely structured as a Mass,[45] a "litany" celebrating the painful and meager existence worked by the Ricketts, the Woods, and the Gudgers upon the inhospitable farmland of Southern Alabama. Agee too celebrates this Mass, for his particular effort at "asserting a symmetry"--which resulted in Let Us Now Praise Famous Men--and because the intensity of his experience with the tenants has been significant for him.[46] Much of this section is addressed directly to the sharecroppers, and this second-person narrative --another narrative innovation--also emphasizes the sense of communion in Agee's experience:

> I remember so well, the first night I
> spent under one of these roofs: We

knew you already, a little, some of
you, most of you: . . . And it was
here that we saw most of you,
scarcely knowing you by families
apart: I can remember it so clearly,
as if it were five minutes ago, and
we were just drawn away from your
company . . .. (361-362)[47]

After this follows a short section entitled "Gradual,"
in which Agee introduces the characters and setting of
the long scene found in a later section entitled
"Introit,"[48] where he recounts his first encounter
with George Gudger and his wife, Annie Mae. Between
these two sections, Agee inserts "Reversion" (372), in
which he describes a trip he and Walker Evans took to
Birmingham halfway through their stay in Alabama. The
trip alienated Agee from the outside world he formerly
knew in a different emotional/psychological context,
and the passage is full of self-conscious anxiety and
sexual frustration, and is obviously meant as a contrast to the warmth and affection of the sharecroppers.
Agee then returns (in "Introit, Parts 1 and 2") to the
incident with George Gudger and his family which he
began in "Gradual." The incident is intensely personal, and completes the reader's introduction to the
Gudger family, which Agee began in "On the Porch: 1."
"Part Three: Inductions" thus comes to an end.

Following a collection of appendices, notes and
reviews, which, as William Stott argues, seems to have
been placed here for no other reason but that they
don't fit anywhere else in the novel,[49] comes the
final section of the text: "On the Porch: 3." In this
last section, Agee returns to the setting and tone of
"On the Porch: 1," but, working from the metafictional
material in "On the Porch: 2," he is now ready to
continue his narrative beyond an introductory point.
Thus, "On the Porch," as Agee indicated in the center
section is, "the beginning of a much longer book" (245).
The novel is in this sense never ending, similar to
the cyclical development of human consciousness. Unlike the conventional realistic novel which conveys an
unchanging empirical reality, consciousness is ever
changing and each writing--each reading--is significantly different:

the form [of Let Us Now Praise Famous
Men] imitates the process of con-

65

sciousness, wherein perception is
sudden inexplicable, quickly lost,
and always beginning again.50

This developing process within the novel also mirrors
the reading process.

In "On the Porch: 3", Agee creates a metaphor for
this subjective process of consciousness, and, thus
concretizes the complex experience of "On the Porch:
2." Agee, Evans and the Gudger family, while lying
on the front porch of the house, listen at dusk51 to
the long, sustained cry of a fox. Agee gives the cry
a musical signature: "-- -- -- --: -- --: -- --:" (464)
and describes how it travels over the countryside,
connecting with a second, a third identical cry (cor-
responding to the three "On the Porch" sections)
which allows it to always remain just beyond his
ability to "trap" it within time and space. The only
discernible difference between the cries is in pitch
and tone, qualities which would change as the listener
changes position. So this becomes the final image for
the novel: a sustained, never specifically locateable
animus which transcends the lives of both Agee and the
tenants, and ultimately, the reader's. This is the
"truth" which Agee believes is the artist's task to
communicate: the "esthetic reality" which both Agee
and the reader have caught in its "most expressive
crystallization"52 and which provides the intensity of
Agee's narrative. He then returns to his argument
that the subjective process in the novel imitates the
process of consciousness; "On the Porch: 3" is the
fullest expression of that process in the novel:

We lay thinking, analyzing, remembering,
in the human and artist's sense praying,
chiefly over matters of the present and
of that immediate past which was a part
of the present; and each of these matters had in that time the extreme
clearness, and edge, and honor, which
I shall now try to give you; until at
length we too fell asleep. [italics
added] (471)

The narrative thus ends with a reference to its
cyclical and subjective structure.

Occasionally, the complexity of Let Us Now Praise

Famous Men obscures Agee's achievement as a novelist.
Since it was published, Agee's novel has troubled both
critic and reviewer; most reviewers of the novel "had
warm praise for the book," but "all were puzzled by
it."[53] Today, however, it is less difficult to perceive the novel as "one of the great nonfictive
narratives . . .."[54] This is especially true in light
of the many other nonfiction novels which have since
followed Let Us Now Praise Famous Men: Norman Mailer's
The Armies of The Night, Of A Fire on the Moon, Miami
and the Siege of Chicago, John Hersey's Hiroshima, The
Algiers Motel Incident, and Tom Wolfe's The Electric
Kool-Aid Acid Test, to name a few of the many American
examples that have been written since 1946. With the
current, large body of criticism about the social and
aesthetic characteristics of modernist literature, the
student of nonfiction is less likely to be "puzzled"
by the novel. Clearly, in addition to being a seminal
text in the development of this subgenre, Let Us Now
Praise Famous Men is a characteristic example of
modernist prose. Thus, the novel, which evolved in
part because of James Agee's insistence upon finding
a suitable literary form for his personal experience
in Alabama, also became the progenitor of a new prose
subgenre which, as will shortly become clear, is still
a vital part of American prose writing.

[1] For an excellent critical history of the period,
see Warren I. Susman, "The Thirties," in The Development of an American Culture, ed. by Stanley Coben and
Lorman Ratner (Englewood Cliffs, N.J.: Prentice-Hall,
Inc., 1970), pp. 179-218. For an informal, oral
history of the period, cf. Hard Times: An Oral History
of The Great Depression, ed. by Studs Terkel (New York:
Avon Books, 1970).

[2] Most notable are, in art: Edward Hopper and
Edward Hartley; in fiction: Micheal Gold, Hemingway,
Agee, Sherwood Anderson, and Henry Roth.

[3] Robert Fitzgerald, "A Memoir," in The Collected
Short Prose of James Agee, ed. by Robert Fitzgerald
(New York: Ballantine Books, 1968), p. 15.

[4] Interestingly, MacDonald would later join Norman
Mailer in 1968, along with poet Paul Goodman, in the
Washington protest March Mailer records in The Armies
of The Night.

[5] Genevieve Moreau, The Restless Journey of James
Agee, trans, by Miriam Kleiger (New York: William
Morrow and Company, 1977), p. 115. Agee later finished
this story, but the manuscript is lost.

[6] Following is the passage from which both the
short story and the novel gain their titles and inspiration:

> "Let us now praise famous men, and our
> fathers that begat us.
> The Lord hath wrought great glory by them
> through his great power from the beginning.
> Such as did bear rule in their kingdoms,
> men renowned for their power, giving counsel
> by their understanding, and declaring
> prophecies:
> Leaders of the people by their counsels,
> and by their knowledge of learning meet
> for the people, wise and eloquent in their

instructions:
Such as found out musical tunes, and
recited verses in writing:
Rich men furnished with ability, living
peaceably in their habitations:
All these were honored in their generations,
and were the glory of their times.
There be of them that have left a name
behind them, that their praises might be
reported.
And some there be which have no memorial;
who perished, as though they had never been;
and are become as though they had never
been born; and their children after them.
But these were merciful men, whose
righteousness hath not been forgotten.
With their seed shall continually remain a
good inheritance, and their children are
within the covenant.
Their seed standeth fast, and their children
for their sakes. Their seed shall remain
forever, and their glory shall not be
blotted out.
Their bodies are buried in peace; but their
name liveth for evermore."

The parallel between much of the punctuation in Let Us Now
Praise Famous Men and in the first half of this
Biblical passage is interesting, especially in the "On
the Porch" sections and the longer section entitled
"Colon". It is also quite clear that the final 12
lines of the passage are those which bear the greatest
meaning for the novel on the Alabama tenant farmers.

[7] cf. Daniel Aaron, Writers On The Left (New York:
Avon Press, 1961) for an adequate history of the
period, and Stott, Documentary Expression and Thirties
America for a superb history of the documentary,
including what might be the best essay on Let Us Now
Praise Famous Men, and certainly the best essay on
Walker Evan's photographs in that novel.

[8] cf. Proletarian Writers of The Thirties, ed. by
David Madden (Carbondale, Ill.: Southern Illinois
University Press, 1968), Introduction. There are some
exceptions to this characterization, however, e.g.,
Jack Conroy, The Disinherited (New York: Atheneum,
1968).

[9]cf. Katerina Clark, The Soviet Novel: History As Ritual (Chicago: University of Chicago Press, 1981), pp. 177-189. Clark's study of the Soviet novel, especially during the 20's and 30's, is excellent, drawing with equal facility from the literature and the history of that turbulent nation.

[10]This is especially the case with Micheal Gold's novel, Jews Without Money.

[11]Stott, p. 298. Note the signals for interpretive "approval" within the documentary: "telegraphing to the audience the feelings it should feel."

[12]Moreau, p. 118.

[13]Stott, pp. 220-225.

[14]James Agee, as quoted in Erling Larson, James Agee (Minneapolis: University of Minnesota Press, 1971), p. 25.

[15]The FSA loaned Evans to Fortune and Agee provided that all of Evan's work would remain theirs; and it has.

[16]The fact that the greatest number of metafictional remarks in the text concern the realistic/naturalistic novel is one more indication that this is the literary form which Agee thought Let Us Now Praise Famous Men most resembled.

[17]Fitzgerald, pp. 45-46, and Stott, pp. 261-263.

[18]The fact that they occur before the title page would support this.

[19]In contrast to Margaret Bourke-White (who is the object of Agee's irony at the end of the text in one of the appendices), Evans let the sharecroppers pose themselves and took their pictures only when they felt comfortable with his doing so.

^{20}Stott, p. 269.

^{21}Book one actually contains three quotes: one
from King Lear, a second, "Workers of the world, unite
and fight. You have nothing to lose but your chains,
and a world to win." which is quoted to "mislead those
who will be misled . . .," and finally, a few passages
from a "third grade geography textbook belonging to
Louise Gudger, aged ten, daughter of a cotton tenant."
The passage from The Communist Manifesto is dealt with
in "Intermission: Conversation in The Lobby," and the
passage from the child's textbook becomes relevant
in the later section called "Education."

^{22}It is interesting to note Agee's conception of
his and Walker Evans's roles in this text, as he
refers to the two of them in the table of characters
as a "spy traveling as a journalist [Agee]" and a
"counterspy, traveling as a photographer [Evans]."
(xxii)

^{23}It is worth noting, however, that this attitude
did not deter him from following through the assignment and attempting to have Fortune publish the
results. He was unsuccessful.

^{24}Fitzgerald, p. 30.

^{25}This same decreasing of the distance between
the author and reader as regards a text was attempted
several years before by both Shklovsky and Lawrence
Sterne in the novel Shklovsky most admired: Tristram
Shandy. Note also that this is very similar to
Brecht's intent in his epischem Theater, and his
theory of the Verfremdungseffekt.

^{26}This is especially true of Margaret Bourke-
White's You Have Seen Their Faces, which more appro-
priately might have been called "You Have Seen My
Faces."

^{27}This is in part suggested by Agee by his
inclusion of the quote from King Lear in Book One.

[28] This was suggested by Agee as well, in the Preamble to the novel (see discussion), and the first critic to have explored this structure at any length is Peter Ohlin: Peter H. Ohlin, _Agee_ (New York: Ivan Obolensky, Inc., 1966), p. 58.

[29] The description of things in these sections bears a marked resemblance to the _chosisme_ technique of description in the _nouveau roman_. cf. Chapter one on the _nouveau roman_.

[30] Zavarzadeh, p. 42.

[31] Stott, p. 311.

[32] This same expression, it will be remembered, was used by Shklovsky to describe his own state of being or consciousness in _A Sentimental Journey_: p. 133.

[33] This passage also points out the validity of our earlier argument about the necessity of changing certain details in the conventional omniscient narrative in order to create and support the personal, subjective conception of the (implied) author. Agee consciously rejects this possibility in _Let Us Now Praise Famous Men_, preferring to include material which identifies him as the intelligence behind the narrative. Agee thus insists on preserving the narrative tension between fictionalization and individuation. This is one important distinction between the nonfiction novel and the conventional realistic novel. Chapter four on Truman Capote's _In Cold Blood_ explores this distinction further.

[34] This point is where Agee senses the distance between the novel (traditional) form and _Let Us Now Praise Famous Men_ is closest, and the passage thus reinforces the argument that the text is legitimately a nonfiction _novel_. It is also clearly not a separate genre.

[35] This point is especially interesting in light of Capote's own work in _In Cold Blood_, where he has imitated the naturalistic writer rather than initiated

a new subgenre of the novel form.

[36]As was demonstrated in Chapter one in the discussion on the _nouveau roman_, even as a pose, objectivity usually indicates and emphasizes its subjective character.

[37]Fitzgerald, p. 39.

[38]Stott, p. 303. Also, the fact that Evans was an avowed homosexual at the time makes this scene even more improbable.

[39]Stott, p. 302.

[40]The change in the project from the original assignment is quite evident here (see quote above), and is largely the reason why _Fortune_ refused to publish the manuscript when Agee returned to New York. As for the connection between Liberalism and the American business community, as well as with the conventional realistic novel, the point has been well made by Zavarzadeh, pp. 27-28.

[41]Agee's anger at bourgeois education, perhaps also at himself for being a product of that system, is clearest on pages 313-315. See also the quote from a child's textbook in Book one of the novel.

[42]"A 'useable past?' (The polite substitute for 'tradition.' Academic; philosophic; critics' language.)" Agee, p. 352. This issue of a "useable past" has been an important one with American critics since the end of the Civil War, and centers on the question of America's emergence as a significant and individual producer of a national literature. cf. Floyd A Stovall, _The Development of American Literary Criticism_ (New Haven: College and University Press, 1955), pp. 38-49.

[43]Note that the transitory quality of these exercises in Agee's maturation is emphasized by the title of the section; "Intermission."

[44] Even the title of these later sections, "Inductions," indicates their subjective quality, which Agee established as the only valid, historical point of view in "On the Porch: 2".

[45] cf. Alfred T. Barson, _A Way of Seeing: A Critical Study of James Agee_ (Amherst: University of Mass. Press, 1972), chapter four.

[46] In his letters to his childhood mentor, Father Flye, Agee suggests that this period was much like the younger years of his Episcopalian childhood, where he felt especially close to those around him. cf. James Agee, _Letters of James Agee to Father Flye_ (New York: Bantom Books, 1963), pp. 11-14.

[47] Following our parallel between the nonfiction novel and the French _nouveau roman_, this same second-person narrative viewpoint was used by some _nouveaux romanciers_: e.g., Michel Butor in _La Modification_.

[48] This is, incidentally, the function of the Gradual in the Episcopalian Mass.

[49] "The whole odd arrangement . . . seems to have been decided on the spur of the moment, in pencil, on a scrap of paper, with casual arrows shifting . . . words about." Stott, p. 310. There is also a sense that these are the last "preliminaries" before Agee begins, for the last time in the novel, "On the Porch" and the novel _per se_. He is, in a sense, "clearing the desk" to begin anew.

[50] Ibid.

[51] This indicates some movement in time, probably twenty-four hours, from "On the Porch: 1," since this first section started in the late evening when Agee was alone.

[52] Fitzgerald, p. 39.

[53] Stott, p. 290.

[54] Zavarzadeh, p. 71

Capote's aim seemed to be to preserve the picture
of the place and of the events before, during and
after the murder, in the way it appeared to everyone
involved or as it might appear to an all-seeing, objective observer--like God, who is clearly not a
novelist. William Phillips

*   *   *

In Cold Blood, like Agee's Let Us Now Praise
Famous Men, also grew out of a magazine assignment
(from The New Yorker), and was published almost in
toto by The New Yorker magazine in 1965, the same year
as Random House published it in book form. But here
the similarity between the two texts ends, despite
Truman Capote's insistence that In Cold Blood is the
first nonfiction novel. In a well publicized interview with George Plimpton in the New York Times Review
of Books (January 16, 1966), Capote described the
"new genre" he had explored in In Cold Blood. Initially, his reason for choosing the subject material
was "purely literary" and was "based on a theory I've
harbored since I first began to write professionally .
. . [:] It seemed to me that journalism, reportage,
could be forced to yield a serious new art form: the
'non-fiction novel', as I thought of it."[1] So, in
order to bring his 'theory' to literary fruition,
Capote proposed a "narrative form that employed all
the techniques of fictional art but was nevertheless
immaculately factual . . . . [italics added]"[2] The
"first essential" embodied in the nonfiction novel is
the "timeless quality about the cause and events."[3]
The subject could not be so immediate and topical that
it would be outdated by the time it was published.
That is, it had to be "typical" enough to outlive the
sensationalism which originally surrounded it. In
addition to fusing factual material with fictional
devices, Capote asserts that "the author should not
appear in the work."[4] This is not to say that the
author does not control the novel's final shape and
"meaning," for, shortly after this remark, Capote
explains:

I make my own comment by what I choose
to tell and how I choose to tell it.
It is true that an author is more in
control of fictional characters because he can do anything he wants with
them as long as they stay credible.
But in the non-fiction novel one can
also manipulate: <u>If I put something in</u>
<u>which I don't agree about I can always</u>
<u>set it in a context of qualification</u>
<u>without having to step into the story</u>
<u>myself to set the reader straight.</u>
[italics added]5

Then, while describing the many interviews and research trips he and his assistant Harper Lee6 conducted for the novel, Capote adds; "I truly don't
believe anything like it [the nonfiction novel] exists
in the history of journalism"7

Thus, Capote argues for his "new form" based on
the "(1) timelessness of the theme; (2) the unfamili-
arity of the setting; and (3) the large cast of
characters that would allow him [Capote] to tell the
story from a variety of points of view", using what
Friedman calls his "Multiple Selective Omniscience."8
And in fact, In Cold Blood follows this formula quite
specifically. However, Capote's theory clearly does
not define a "new" nonfiction genre, but rather merely
repeats most of the qualities of the conventional
realistic novel. Moreover, In Cold Blood does not
even follow Capote's "definition" in one major regard:
that of complete, "immaculate" factuality. Research
has shown that Capote added and changed important
details of the Clutter murder, in spite of his nearly
six years of research for the novel. Alone, this
point does not refute Capote's claim that the novel is
a nonfiction text, but it does draw our attention to
the contrast between the nonfiction novel and the
conventional novel. By changing major details in the
novel and by using the omniscient narrator typical of
the realistic novel, Capote creates the "shared
reality" which Damian Grant argues convincingly is the
epistemological foundation of the conventional novel.9
Understanding these dimensions in In Cold Blood is
important because both Capote's definition and his
novel have become accepted as the critical archetype
for the nonfiction novel in American nonfiction
criticism. Even in The Mythopoeic Reality, M. Zavarzadeh

calls In Cold Blood "one of the achieved nonfiction novels written in the postwar years,"[10] apparently unaware that many points between Capote's definition and in the novel do not coincide; in fact, Capote's definition conflicts with both Zavarzadeh's description of the nonfiction novel and our own. Thus, in addition to demonstrating that In Cold Blood does not follow Capote's own "definition" of the nonfiction novel, we can show that a.) Capote's description is not adequate to define the nonfiction novel, and b.) that In Cold Blood is a conventional realistic novel based on an actual historical occurrence.

The historical murders occured on November 15, 1959, and involved four prominent Kansas victims--the Clutter family: father, mother, son and daughter--and two murderers, Perry Smith and Richard Hickock. But, the senselessness and brutality of these murders[11] draws them apart from similar crimes which are more easily explained and accepted. In fact, from a novelist's point of view, the lack of a plausible motive for the Clutter murders must have been inviting. The lack of a rational or "acceptable" motive for these murders and the visciousness with which they were carried out makes them grotesque and nearly ritualistic.[12] This dimension helps to create the timeless quality Capote described earlier, since the murders violate something larger and more fundamental than the individual lives of the Clutter family: the American Ideal archetype.[13] Secondly, the setting of the crime--Holcomb, Kansas--although it is stereotypical "middle America," is certainly unfamiliar to the majority of Capote's readers, in part because Capote de-emphasizes the specific location and underscores its typicality.[14] The murder site, a prosperous wheat farm built from Herb Clutter's hard work and sound business sense, helps create the timelessness of Capote's subject matter, since it strikes the very heart of the American middle class archetype. Finally, Capote uses several narrative viewpoints ("centres of consciousness") to tell his story, most of them secondary: for example, Larry Hendrick's narrative presented in the section entitled "The Last to See Them Alive"[15] is narrated in a voice never heard again in the novel. Hendricks, an English teacher and aspiring fiction writer, presents the first coherent account of the discovery of the murdered Clutter family, which, significantly, Capote indicated in his interview required a "slight editing job."[16] The

three major narrative perspectives are those of the
two murderers Perry Smith and Richard Hickock and of
their determined Kansas Bureau of Investigation pur-
suer, Alvin Dewey.[17] The novel opens from the
omniscient point of view of the "implied author;"[18]
that is, the narrative voice closest to the intelligence behind the novel: "The village of Holcomb stands
on the high wheat plains of western Kansas, a lonesome
area that other Kansans call 'out there'" (3), and
ends from the perspective of the exhausted but victor-
iours Alvin Dewey:[19]

> "And nice to have seen you, Sue. Good
> Luck," he called after her as she dis-
> appeared down the path, a pretty girl
> in a hurry, her smooth hair swinging,
> shining--just such a woman as Nancy
> might have been. Then, starting home,
> he walked toward the trees and under
> them, leaving behind him the big sky,
> the whisper of the wind voices in the
> wind bent wheat. (343)

These three narrative points of view are at opposite
ends of the novel: Smith and Hickock on the "other
side" of the law, Alvin Dewey on the side of the law
and order, which, as in the American crime novel
tradition (not to mention the American western), must
finally be victorious.

Thus, Capote has followed his formula closely--
especially as regards form--but clearly the formula
describes the conventional realistic novel, not the
nonfiction novel. The typical setting is characteristic of the shared reality conveyed in the conventional
novel. Capote also utilizes a number of "centres of
consciousness", by which he provides the reader with
"another perspective"[20] of the murders and their con-
sequences. Finally, Capote uses a neutral omniscient
narrator who is unidentified and whose relationship to
the text is that of an "implied author," a role which
Wayne Booth discussed essentially within the conventional novel.[21] This nameless, God-like narrative
intelligence perceives a certain irony and form within
the murders and structures the novel to share this
"unified meaning"[22] with the reader. While such a
unified conception can also be found in the nonfiction
novel, no attempt is made in In Cold Blood--unlike in
the nonfiction form--to provide specific details and

information about the narrating personality, as was
true with both A Sentimental Journey and Let Us Now
Praise Famous Men. The novel provides no knowledge
about the narrating intelligence which would help the
reader understand the subjective structuring of the
novel. In Cold Blood retains the aesthetic and
authorial distance of the conventional realistic novel;
it "is that old'fashioned spellbinding kind of 'novel'
that draws us out of ourselves and into the shaped
world of the storyteller."[23]

Thus, until the point when Smith and Hickock are
finally apprehended by Dewey and his men (p. 215), the
narrative progresses along two parallel lines: one
level concerning Smith and Hickock alternates with a
second narrative level about the events and the personalities in Holcomb (including Dewey). For example,
on page thirteen, Herb Clutter allows a group of
Oklahoma hunters to hunt on his land, then heads for
home, "unaware that . . . [today] would be his last."
On the following page the next section begins, with
the words, "Like Mr. Clutter, the young man breakfast-
ing in the cafe [Perry Smith] called the Little Jewel
never drank coffee. (14)" The author's arrangement
here is obvious. The reader is provided a simultaneity
of action which is unavailable to any of the characters,
except, of course, to the omniscient narrator (who is,
Wayne Booth argues, a character[24]). The story
moreover, may never have occurred exactly as Capote
has arranged it. Nearly every section is juxtaposed
with the preceding one in order to underscore the
"arrangement" and coincidence between them and, to
create a pointed irony which pervades the murder sequence. Another instance involves Herbert Clutter's
brother, who, voicing the paranoia which has crept
into the lives of Holcomb's citizens, says to a
reporter shortly after the funeral:

> When this is cleared up, I'll wager
> whoever did it [the murders] was
> someone within ten miles of where
> we now stand. (88)

The next section on Smith and Hickock begins with:

> Approximately four hundred miles
> east of where Arthur Clutter then
> stood, two young men [Smith and
> Hickock] were sharing a booth in

                    the Eagle Buffet, a Kansas City
                    Diner. (89)

And later, when the two murderers are about to be
picked up, Perry Smith wanders into a Las Vegas post
office to pick up a package he had mailed to himself
from Mexico. As he and Hickock leave with the box of
Smith's personal belongings,

                    Neither . . . was aware of the police
                    vehicle trailing them as they pulled
                    away from the post office . . . they
                    traveled five blocks north, . . .
                    and stopped in front of a dying palm
                    tree and a weather-wrecked sign from
                    which calligraphy had faded except
                    the word "OOM." "This it?" Dick asked.
                    Perry, as the patrol car drew along-
                    side, nodded. (215)

The important point is that the narrator creates a
certain irony by consciously structuring and arranging
these random, almost accidental events. He supplies
the symmetry and form which the murders themselves
lacked at the time. This is similar to many other
traditional novels which utilize historical material'
for example, Dostoevsky's Crime and Punishment, especially, and The Possessed, where the historical
material is incidental to the fictional arrangement
and intent of the novel.[25] Thus Capote's novel is
not a nonfiction novel, but is conventional realistic
(historical) fiction. The narrative points of view,
the typicalizing of the setting, and the omniscient
narrator are essential features of the conventional
novel, and are the specific characteristics against
which the nonfiction novel, especially Agee's Let Us
Now Praise Famous Men, developed. According to John
Hollowell, although "Capote insisted upon the factual
accuracy of all the situations and dialogue that he
depicted, his narrative read more like a novel than a
historical account."[26] This is exactly the issue, for
Capote has simply used historical material in much the
same way as the Nineteenth Century Realists did and
has done his job well.

        One final point requires explanation to show the
contrast more sharply. One quality which Capote insisted upon in his description of the nonfiction novel
was its factual quality. And yet, this is the only

part of his description which he did not follow. In
his interview for the New York Times Review of Books,
Capote described the material--in In Cold Blood as
"immaculately factual." Later in the same interview,
he added: "One doesn't spend almost six years on a
book, the point of which is factual accuracy, and then
give way to minor distortions."[27] We would expect the
historical material in the nonfiction novel to be
"immaculately factual," down to the most insignificant
detail. But this is not the case with In Cold Blood.
Several sections of the novel which certainly would
have been clarified in Capote's six years of research
have been altered, many of them to heighten the irony
and resolution of the novel. Without a specifically
identified voice to report events in the novel, the
narrator in In Cold Blood selects and arranges the
material to most "convincingly embody" the novelist's
"interpretation of the 'human condition'" and thus
provide the text with "credibility and internal believability."[28] This process of altering specific
events to make them typical seems characteristic of
the traditional omniscient narrative,[29] and is certainly true in Capote's novel. In a nonfiction novel,
the identity of the narrator as a character in the
text decreases the distance between the implied author
and the text, and minimizes the amount of distortion,
or in Agee's terms, "falsifying", which oftens occurs
in an omniscient narrative.

There are three significant passages in the novel
which have been invented or altered. The first concerns the actual point at which Perry Smith confesses
the four murders. In the novel, Smith confesses out
of anger in a car with detective Alvin Dewey over a
story which Smith had told Dick Hickock in private.
The story told how Smith murdered a black man in prison
without justification, and when Dewey reveals this
information to Smith to prove that Hickock had already
confessed:

> [The] prisoner gasps. He twists around
> in his seat until he can see . . . the
> motorcade's second car, see inside it:
> "The tough boy! . . . I thought it was
> a real stunt. I didn't believe you.
> That Dick let fly. The tough Boy! . . .
> So Dick was afraid of me? That's amus-
> ing. I'm very amused. What he don't
> know is, I almost did shoot him." Dewey

> lights two cigarettes, one for him-
> self, one for the prisoner. "Tell
> us about it, Perry." (232-233)

Following this, Perry tells the gruesome tale to Dewey
in a fashion which is almost stereotypical melodrama,
and incidentally, which is completely consistent with
the crime movie/novel convention which flourished in
the U.S. during the 1940's and 1950's.[30] In fact,
however, Capote's version of this scene seems not to
have been the case at all. In the official transcript
of the trial, specifically in the testimony of Alvin
Dewey, several different points are established: 1)
that Perry Smith had begun to "crack" in the Las Vegas
City Jail and didn't confess for the first time in the
car; 2) that Smith and Dewey were not in the lead car
as Capote describes it, but in the last car where Smith
would have seen nothing but highway had he turned
around; and more importantly, 3) that it was not the
prison story which brought on Smith's final confession,
but rather Dewey's revelation of Hickock's statements
during interrogation.[31] After hearing that Hickock
denied killing any of the Clutters, Smith actually
said that "that isn't right . . . He killed two and I
killed two."[32] Thus, much significant information
in this passage seems to be less than "immaculately
factual."

     The second difficulty concerns the auctioning
of the Clutter equipment and belongings after Smith
and Hickock have been apprehended. Specifically,
the passage describes the auctioning of Nancy Clutter's
pet horse, Babe:

> "I hear fifty . . . sixty-five . . .
> seventy . . .": the bidding was
> laggardly, nobody seemed really to
> want Babe, and the man who got her,
> a Mennonite farmer who said he might
> use her for plowing, paid seventy
> five dollars. As he led her out of
> the corral, Sue Kidwell ran forward;
> she raised her hand as though to wave
> goodbye, but instead clapped it over
> her mouth. (271)

Again, as with the confession scene, the sale of the
horse is very emotional and melodramatic, designed to
increase the reader's sympathy for the Clutter family.

Selling Nancy Clutter's pet horse for a mere seventy-
five dollars, and the stifled emotion of Nancy's best
friend, Sue Kidwell, would certainly elicit the pathos
Capote wants before the trial scenes. The passage
confirms the vitality of the American archetype, the
American Dream which the Clutter murders, the reader
now realizes, fundamentally threatens.[33] In fact,
however, the horse was not sold for a mere seventy-five
dollars, nor was it sold to a Mennonite farmer. The
man who bought the horse was Mr. Seth Earnest, the
postmaster's father, who paid a fair $182.50 for her.
Further, Babe is not being used to plow anything, but
is used instead to train Y.M.C.A. children to ride.[34]
One significance of this "minor interpolation" is that
"it provides the flourish Capote needed to complete
short story number seventy."[35] The specific issue is
that, again, the actual account differs quite radically from Capote's fictional record.

Finally, towards the end of the murder trial,
Capote shows Smith becoming close to Mrs. Meier, the
wife of the jailer in Garden City, Kansas, where the
trial is being conducted. In the sixty-fifth chapter
of the novel, which is told from her point of view,
Mrs. Meier states:

> I heard him [Smith] crying. I turned
> on the radio. Not to hear him. But
> I could. Crying like a child. He'd
> never broke down before, shown any
> sign of it. Well, I went to him. The
> door of his cell. He reached out his
> hand. He wanted me to hold his hand,
> and I did, I held his hand, and all
> he said was, "I'm embraced by shame."
> (308)

In an interview with Phillip K. Tompkins on February
26, 1966, Mrs. Meier "insisted that this incident had
never taken place--and that she had not told Capote
any such thing."[36] Again, Capote has created a highly
emotional scene which differs from actual fact, and
which is far from being "immaculately factual." Instead,
the scene helps create narrative sympathy for Perry
Smith throughout the last part of the novel.

Many other incidents in the novel are apparently
less than completely accurate: for example, the
account of Perry Smith's last words. Before he ascends

the gallows, Smith reportedly says:

> I think . . . it's a helluva thing
> to take a life in this manner. I
> don't believe in capital punishment,
> morally or legally. Maybe I had
> something to contribute, something--
> . . . It would be meaningless to
> apologize for what I did. Even
> inappropriate. But I do. I apolo-
> gize. (340)

In fact, the official record shows that Smith never
apologized.[37] These and other passages not only
indicate that Capote exaggerated and embellished
actual events to increase the emotional and melodramatic quality of his best selling novel, but they also
provide one important distinction between the nonfiction novel and the conventional realistic novel. In
the conventional realistic novel, the historical
material is subordinate to the perceptual structure
of the narrative intelligence. The omniscient narrative precludes the personal, autobiographical material
required by the bifurcated narrative structure of the
nonfiction novel. Clearly, <u>In Cold Blood</u> is a conventional realistic novel and is not the prose innovation its author claimed. For Capote's claims at the
time the novel was published, such historical
"inaccuracy . . . is of course devastating."[38]

[1] Plimpton, p. 25.

[2] Ibid., p. 26.

[3] Ibid., p. 38.

[4] Ibid., p. 32.

[5] Plimpton, p. 32.

[6] Herself an author of a Pulitzer Prize novel, To Kill a Mockingbird.

[7] Plimpton, p. 28.

[8] Friedman, pp. 127-128, and Hollowell, p. 64.

[9] Grant, p. 9.

[10] Zavarzadeh, p. 115. This also reflects the misconception which still persists in American criticism that In Cold Blood was the first nonfiction novel. Ronald Weber apparently assumes the same thing about In Cold Blood, referring to it as an archetype of the form.

[11] All told, the two men killed the entire Clutter family for less than $100 in cash and goods.

[12] For example, this same quality exists in E.A. Poe's The Murders in the Rue Morgue, where a murder which defies any kind of logical explanation acquires a timeless grotesque quality. cf. Robert A. Smart, "The Rhetoric of the Grotesque: E.A. Poe and Franz Kafka," Thesis University of Utah, 1977, Chapters one and two.

[13] Grotesque and ritualistic murder nearly always carries this timeless mythic dimension. cf. Arnold

Heidsieck, <u>Das Groteske und das Absurde im modernen Drama</u>, (Stuttgart: Kohlhammer, 1979,) Chapter one.

[14]Like most mythical archetypes, either no one <u>really</u> lives there, or the place really doesn't exist. It is usually a contrasting ideal to everyone's "normal" life which embodies the values of the cultural majority. This is the quality Capote wishes to draw out of his picture of Holcomb. cf. the popular American film which also uses Kansas as a setting: <u>The Wizard of Oz</u> and the recent ABC Kansas "docudrama" set in Lawrence, Kansas, <u>The Day After</u>.

[15]Truman Capote, <u>In Cold Blood</u> (New York: Random House, 1965), pp. 61-66. All subsequent references will be from this edition.

[16]Plimpton, p. 31. We are reminded of Shklovsky's comment about Lazar Zervandov's manuscript at the end of <u>A Sentimental Journey</u>.

[17]The stereotypical quality of this reworked, nearly clichéd <u>revenge tale</u> (cf. p. 80, <u>In Cold Blood</u>) is never very subtle throughout the novel; Capote seems to affirm the myth of the justice of the American West, that justice will always prevail, as a part of a shared American reality.

[18]Booth, pp. 71-76. This role is also strongly intimated in Capote's interview comment on p. 76 of this study.

[19]Whose voice by this time is nearly identical with the implied author's.

[20]Which the nonfiction novelist would maintain is impossible.

[21]Obviously, we can describe an implied author for the nonfiction novel, since the novel is being written at some different time, at some different place, by some different person; but the point is--as we indicated in Chapter one--that the sympathetic and aesthetic distance between the implied author and the text (character/narrator) is consciously much narrower

in the nonfiction novel than in the conventional realistic novel.

[22] Zavarzadeh, p. 41.

[23] Weber, p. 73.

[24] Booth, p. 273.

[25] The historical component of The Possessed has already been noted, but the historical currency which Dostoevsky interwove throughout Crime and Punishment is also quite important to a full understanding of that novel. cf. Richard Peace, Dostoevsky: An Examination of the Major Novels (Cambridge University Press, 1970), pp. 22-23. cf. also Tony Tanner, "On the Parapet," in Will The Real Norman Mailer Please Stand Up, ed. by Laura Adams (Port Washington, NY: Kennikat Press, 1974), p. 116.

[26] Hollowell, p. 63.

[27] Plimpton, p. 39.

[28] Zavarzadeh, p. 77.

[29] cf. Booth, pp. 156-157, and Friedman, pp. 110, 119, and 124.

[30] cf. Tough Guy Writers of the Thirties, ed. by David Madden (Carbondale: Southern Illinois University Press, 1967), Introduction. This form was a modification of the Elizabethan revenge tragedy, where one character emerged from an anarchic state of political and ethical/moral disarray as the representative of society and justice and so became its agent to "right" things. He would achieve this at the cost of many lives, and affirm the harmony and design of the world. cf. John Webster's The Duchess of Malfi for a typical example.

[31] Phillip K. Tompkins, "In Cold Fact," In Truman Capote's In Cold Blood: A Critical Handbook, ed. by Irving Malin (Belmont, Cal.: Wadsworth Publishing Co., 1968), pp. 48-49.

[32] Ibid., p. 49.

[33] For if, as in the Elizabethan revenge tragedy, justice does not prevail and revenge is not gained (to affirm the divine harmony and symmetry of the universe), then the universe will be shown to be absurd. Also, as will be shown in the following chapter, the same process operates in Mailer's *Execution-er's Song* between the Mormon culture and G. Gilmore.

[34] Tompkins, pp. 45-56.

[35] Ibid., p. 46.

[36] Ibid., p. 52.

[37] Ibid., pp. 53-54.

[38] Weber, p. 74.

CHAPTER FIVE:

NORMAN MAILER: THE ARMIES OF THE NIGHT
AND EXECUTIONER'S SONG

I was brought up on the idea that when you wrote
a novel you tried to build a character who could be
handled and walked around like a piece of sculpture. .
. . It made me decide there's no clear boundary
between experience and imagination.   Norman Mailer

I like language, but I tell the truth.   Gary
Gilmore

*   *   *

The Armies of The Night

The Armies of The Night is one of three nonfiction novels which are a personal record of Norman
Mailer's political activities during the 1960's: The
Armies of The Night (1968), Miami and The Siege of
Chicago (1968), and Of A Fire on The Moon (1970).   The
three novels together "comprise a kind of impression-
istic history of the sixties seen through the distorting
lens of a participant-observer."[1]   Of the three texts,
The Armies of The Night is the most significant, since
it was Mailer's first nonfiction novel, and because in
it he makes the clearest attempt to distinguish and
define the nonfiction sub-genre.   The Armies of The
Night was written at a time in Mailer's artistic
development when his roles as writer and social
activist became fused, and he considered the nonfiction
novel the form best suited for writing about a constantly fluctuating, revolutionary society.   In the
words of Laura Adams:

> [It is] as if Mailer at this point
> began to suspect that the novel, the
> poem, the story--the conventional
> literary genres to which he had de-
> voted so much of his talent and
> energy--were no longer capable of
> influencing the masses, and that the
> revolution in the consciousness of our

89

time would have to be abandoned or
approached through radically different
means.[2]

The historical and formal parallels between The Armies
of The Night and Agee's Let Us Now Praise Famous Men
are suggestive for our understanding of the nonfiction
novel.[3] The historical parallels between the two
texts illustrate the modernist quality of nonfiction,
specifically, the idea that the nonfiction novel (and
all modernist literature) is one response to a trau-
matic and changing historical universe.[4] The formal
or aesthetic parallels between the two novels suggest
that the nonfiction novel is a stable and cohesive
subgenre of the novel and that our description of it
is essentially correct. Like Let Us Now Praise Famous
Men, The Armies of The Night is a nonfiction novel,
and belongs within the description provided in Chapter
one. Both nonfiction novels were written at a significant transition point in each author's life, when
each writer blurred the traditional distance between
art and life to become a participant-observer in a
novel which he was writing. Historically, the United
States was under similar political and cultural
pressures: in the 1930's, the American Left (of which
Agee was an active member) was the most active new
political and cultural element in the country; in the
decade from 1960 to 1970, leftist movements were active
throughout the United States, especially on college
campuses. This active protest (mostly against the
Johnson Administration)[5] crossed every cultural, political, ethnic and racial boundary in the United States.
It was this particular protest which Mailer joined,
and The Armies of The Night is his first of a three
volume "history" of that activist period. Both novels
were written at a point in each author's life when
certain personal values were scrutinized and eventually
changed. Interestingly, once each man became less
active socially and politically, each returned to more
conventional literary and artistic forms.[6]

Subtitled "History as a Novel, the Novel as
History," The Armies of The Night is divided into two
parts, with the first and longest book entitled
"History as a Novel: The Steps of the Pentagon," and
the second, shorter book entitled "The Novel as History: The Battle of the Pentagon." Both sections of
the novel correspond to the two sections in A Sentimental Journey: the second part in each parodies the

conventional novel form. The novel details Mailer's
involvement in a large, organized march on the Pentagon
in October, 1967, and includes his arrest, confinement,
and release following the protest demonstration. Book
one is a personal narrative concerning Mailer's
activities and reflections before, during, and after
the march. Book two presents an "objective" and larger
perspective of the same activity which fills in the
broader, "historical" material which would be unavailable to any participant in the march. Both parts of
The Armies of The Night, although not integrated into
a structure as complex as both major sections of Let
Us Now Praise Famous Men,[7] counterpoint in the same
fashion to achieve the same result: both novels parody
the conventional forms to move beyond them toward the
nonfiction novel. Book one is narrated from the perspective of Norman Mailer as participant, and book two
is narrated from the omniscient perspective of the
conventional realistic novel. Thus in book two Mailer
attempts to structure his personal experience during
the march into a shared, "totalized" perspective. Also
in book two, Mailer demonstrates that an omniscient,
"objective" narrative is inappropriate for his purpose,
which is to record a personal "history" of the Pentagon
march. He then focuses on the nature and design of
the nonfiction novel, and suggesting clearly that
nonfiction has become an important dimension of post
war American prose.

The novel opens with a map of the Pentagon's
Washington grounds, detailing all the access roads and
parking lots: in short, every geographic location
which will figure in the novel is represented here.
Following the title page, Mailer reproduces a Time
magazine excerpt from the October 27, 1967 issue,
which recounts his drunken performance at a protest
rally the evening before. The article is unflattering
and is followed by Mailer's statement that now "we may
leave Time in order to find out what happened."[8] The
implication is clearly that the "truth" is not dis-
cerned by the "objective" eye of the observer[9] (i.e.,
the Time reporter who was present), but rather through
the eye of the participant-observer-recorder. Thus
the traditional distance between the text and the
author is narrowed, leading Mailer to ask "how can one
know the truth if one has not experienced it or if one
does not share the novelist's gift of intuition and
his feeling for nuance."[10] In this remark, "the
novelist" probably refers to Mailer personally, since

he uses the term to refer to himself several times in the novel.[11] From the beginning, Mailer refuses to adopt the omniscient pose of the conventional realistic novel and openly maintains the validity of his own subjective perspective. In Book one, Mailer explores the antipathy between the conventional narrative and the nonfiction narrative, thus revealing the metafictionality which is characteristic of the nonfiction sub-genre. Specifically, Mailer focuses on the "typical" narration of the conventional novel, and the reader's expectations of conventional fiction. Thus, the two narrative planes woven through The Armies of The Night are Norman Mailer's activities and personal thoughts during the Washington march, and, secondly, the theoretical material contrasting the conventional realistic novel and the nonfiction novel. Between these, Norman Mailer's role(s) guides the reader from book one to book two and, ultimately, to the resolution of the novel.

In contrast to Let Us Now Praise Famous Men, The Armies of The Night is narrated from a third person omniscient point of view, and the protagonist is Norman Mailer, character/participant:

> On a day somewhat early in September, the year of the first march on the Pentagon, 1967, the phone rang one morning and Norman Mailer, operating on his own principle of war games and random play, picked it up.[12] (14)

To make sure, however, that the relationship of Norman Mailer (as a character) to the narrator is clear, Mailer refers to himself in the beginning as "The Historian (24)" and throughout the remaining text as "The Novelist (37)." Mailer also calls himself "The Beast (43)", "The Existentialist (53)", "General Mailer (133)", and significantly, "The Participant (152)." Each new title appears after Mailer has just described his thoughts ("Existentialist") or referred to how he is often characterized publically ("Beast") or just after he redefines his role in the novel: "Novelist", "Historian", and "Participant." Thus, one of the important aspects of Mailer's novel in particular and of the nonfiction sub-genre generally is his protean role within it: he very clearly identifies himself as the author, narrator, and main character of the text.

As we mentioned earlier, certain metafictional passages in book one point out the differences between the conventional novel and the nonfiction novel. Specifically, Mailer-narrator refers to the reader's expectations of the conventional realistic novel. This is reminiscent of Agee's point in Let Us Now Praise Famous Men, that the reader of the conventional novel is "so used to the idea that art is a fiction that he can't shake himself of it." The term "fiction" as Mailer uses it in The Armies of The Night refers to the "typification" required by the use of an omniscient narrator. As our discussion of Capote's In Cold Blood showed, changing a personal experience into a typical or "totalized" one (in the traditional realistic novel) requires a certain amount of fictionalizing, or in this case, "typicalizing." If the aesthetic goal of the realistic-naturalistic novel--verisimili-tude, "vraisemblance"--is sought, then some details which are part of the shared reality between reader and the writer[13] will replace personal details in the experience which are too private and which are less likely to affirm the universe held commonly by the reader and the writer. This seems a necessary process in creating a typical realistic novel.[14] Mailer considers this process in the course of the novel. Early in the novel, for example, Mailer-narrator des-cribes a party held before the march on Washington, at which most of the liberal activists are present. However, most of the first page is used to detail Mailer-character's ambivalent feelings about this kind of party, until the narrator interrupts his internal dialogue with: "But we are back with the wives, and the room has not yet been described." (25) This is a clear reference to the usual manner of engaging the reader in a shared experience within the conventional realistic or historical novel: the narrator first describes the milieu, the characters, and then presents dialogue. Later, as Mailer-narrator nears the end of this section, he states: "Of course, if this were a novel, Mailer would spend the rest of the night with a lady. . . . Rather he can leave such matters to the happy or unhappy imagination of the reader." (66) Both these passages draw the attention to the novel convention and to our conventional reading expecta-tions of that form; the first passage parodies the objective description of milieu characteristic of the realistic novel. By "baring the device," the second passage parodies a type of conventional novel still popular in the United States at the time The Armies of

The Night was published: the paperback fictions which claim to show a "slice of life," but which are also replete with sexual material to increase sales.[15] Although it is a topical reference, Mailer's point is nonetheless relevant to his distinction between the nonfiction novel and the realistic novel. The reader of such popular and conventional fiction would conceivably expect--both of the novel and of Mailer[16]--a scene in which Mailer the character went to bed with a woman. Mailer parodies and violates these conventional expectations in order to emphasize the uniqueness of the Washington march. So, following these passages, Mailer tells the reader how difficult it is to narrate such "an ambiguous event"; the implication is that all events are ambiguous, contrary to the assumption behind the "objective pose" of the conventional novel, and so can only be narrated from a subjective and clearly identified perspective like that in the non-fiction novel. The distance between Mailer (implied author) and the text is considerably closer than it would be in a conventional novel, and from this changed relationship comes his difficulty in narrating the Washington march from the conventional omniscient perspective which he has just parodied. Mailer's roles as Partipant, Narrator, and (implied) Novelist tend to be identical, thus making it difficult for him to separate his personality within the narrative from the "real" Norman Mailer, or at least from Norman Mailer at the time he wrote The Armies of The Night.[17] Thus, following his remarks on the conventional novel, Mailer parodies the character-persona choice which would be necessary in the traditional novel:[18]

> For that, an eyewitness who is a parti-
> cipant but not a vested partisan is
> required, further he must be not only
> involved, but ambiguous in his own
> proportions, a comic hero, which is to
> say, one cannot happily resolve the
> emphasis of the category--is he finally
> comic, a ludricrous figure with mock-
> heroic associations; or is he not
> unheroic, and therefore embedded some-
> what tragically in the comic? (67)

The issue in Mailer's argument is that within the nonfiction novel, the most valid and legitimate narrative point of view identifies the implied author with the narrator-character. The only "accurate" perspective

is a subjective one: "Once History inhabits a crazy
house [as in the U.S. in 1967], egotism may be the
last tool left to History." (58)" With that, Mailer-
character, "the narrative vehicle" for the Pentagon
march, returns to the historical events of the march.

Thus the narrative in book one, "History as a
Novel" contains Mailer's subjective record of his
activities and observations during a three to four day
period which includes the Pentagon march and his
imprisonment, and which is interwoven with parodies
of the conventional historical novel form. The subjective account and metafictional qualities which
distinguish the nonfiction novel from the traditional
novel are obvious. Aside from his comments on what
he sees as America's ("Cancer Gulch") fatal flaw (the
increasing identification of the military as the
Christian arm of the country, p. 320) and the fact
that the most serious symptom of that flaw is the
Vietnam conflict, Mailer also explores the need for a
nonfiction form. This exploration began in book one,
but the distinction between the existing, traditional
form and the nonfiction novel is not clearly drawn
until book two, "The Novel as History."

On the last page of book one, Mailer describes
his task to the reader:

> Then he [Mailer] began his history of
> the Pentagon. It insisted on becoming
> a history of himself over four days,
> and therefore was history in the costume
> of the novel. He labored in the aesthe-
> tic of the problem for weeks, discovering
> that his dimensions as a character were
> simple: blessed had been the novelist,
> for his protagonist was a simple of a
> hero and a marvel of a fool, with more
> than average gifts of objectivity. . .
> This verdict, disclosed by the unprotec-
> tive haste with which he was obliged to
> write, . . . as if the accelerating
> history of the country forbade deliber-
> ation. (241)

The historical significance of the nonfiction form is
indicated in the last sentence of this passage. For
Mailer, history is no longer knowable, is no longer
expressed in terms of generally accepted epistemological

beliefs, and the nonfiction subgenre is its most appropriate literary representation. Book one also ends with a reference to the _Time_ magazine article about Mailer's "scatalogical solo at the Ambassador Theatre" which began the novel. Clearly <u>now</u>, the reader knows what actually happened after his decision to join the Pentagon marchers.

Book two begins by describing for several pages the many machinations and negotiations required to stage this "historical event." The personae are identified, the negotiations described, and all the logistics are related to the reader in traditional "journalistic" style:

> At this point, Dellinger [the march organizer] called in Jerry Rubin from Berkeley to be Project Director for the march. Rubin had enormous stature among youth groups and Under-Thirties, second perhaps only to Mario Savio. Rubin had organized Vietnam Day at Berkeley (the first mass protest of the war) had led marches in Berkeley designed to block troop trains, then massive marches in Oakland, had served a thirty-day jail sentence, and had appeared at a House Un-American Activities Committee hearing in an American Revolutionary War uniform. (251)

The prose is almost completely free of personal inflection and comment, and Mailer's intention is to inform rather than to recreate the author's "self" in the material.[19] Much of the first part of book two is related in this manner until Chapter six begins: "It is on this particular confrontation [between the marchers and the military[20]] that the conceit one is writing a history must be relinquished. (283)" Then, Mailer adds: "It is obvious the first book is a history in the guise or dress or manifest of a novel, and the second is a real or true novel—no less!— presented in the style of a history." (284) Neither form—history nor novel—can present an objective account of experience; they become "guises" or "poses." Only the personal perspective in book one is legitimate and nondeceptive. In fact, Mailer's position here is consistent with the argument he prepared in book one. Because the only accurate—i.e., "real"—

history is one mediated through a subjective point of view, then the novel itself is a history—both subjective and personal—since it is also a novel: "History as a Novel." The novel in general—both nonfiction and conventional (even though the latter "poses" objectivity)—is a subjective form, like all literature and art:

> The novel is a form of fiction and as such it is _imaginative_. No matter how realistic the manner, how historical the material, the imaginative conceptions of the author are always woven, as woof on warp, on the background of truth to nature and truth to history and truth to life. Again, the novel is based on human experience.[21]

Powerful and personally experienced history, Mailer suggests, should be recorded through a subjective form such as the nonfiction novel. "Objective" recreation of the material requires objective sounding language ("the style of a history"), but does not alter the subjective nature of the material. This is probably the reason for Mailer's return to the personal narrative of book one, after he has explained this point to the reader (283). And "history", as Mailer uses it in the first part of book two, is basically equivalent to the conventional realistic novel, since both forms are based on the same epistemological assumptions:

> history is interior—no documents can give sufficient intimation: the novel must replace history at precisely that point where experience is sufficiently emotional, spiritual, physical, moral, existential, or supernatural to expose the fact that the historian in pursuing the experience would be obliged to quit the clearly demarcated limits of historic inquiry. (284)

It is important that the individual quality of this material be maintained, and one form which allows this is the nonfiction novel. Thus, Mailer's activities in Washington emerged as a different literary form than did Truman Capote's experience with the Clutter murders. The same is not true, however of another text by Mailer which has recently been compared to <u>In Cold Blood</u> as a nonfiction novel: Mailer's account of the Gary Gilmore execution.

<u>The Armies of The Night</u>, however, does fit our description of the nonfiction novel. Like both <u>A Sentimental Journey</u> and <u>Let Us Now Praise Famous Men</u>, Mailer's novel recounts a specific historical event in which the narrator and main character played an actual role. Thus, the implied author, narrator, and character are identical; the distance between the author and the text is reduced, allowing such a close identification of roles. In addition, much of the novel, especially book one, contains specific information about Norman Mailer's personality, since the view or perception which is recorded is personal and not typical. Mailer's personality is also thrust between the fictional devices he uses and the reader of <u>The Armies of The Night</u>. And, finally, as with the other nonfiction novels we have discussed, <u>The Armies of The Night</u> is clearly metafictional: within the narrative, Mailer distinguished it from other existing forms, especially the traditional realistic novel. It is not difficult to see the parallels between the novels of Shklovsky, Agee and Mailer, as well as the contrasts between them and Truman Capote's <u>In Cold Blood</u> and, recently Mailer's <u>Executioner's Song</u>.

Executioner's Song

We noted earlier that The Armies of The Night is the first in a triptych of nonfiction novels which recounts Mailer's political activism in the 1960's. After he finished Of A Fire On The Moon, Mailer followed different creative directions, notably film-making (Maidstone, 1968) and criticism (Genius and Lust, 1976). It was not until 1979 that Mailer pro-duced a text which again drew attention to the nonfiction subgenre which he had explored ten years earlier. Based on the January 17, 1977 firing squad execution of convicted killer Gary Gilmore in the Utah State prison, Executioner's Song once again drew attention to the nonfiction novel, and so invites some consideration here. Actually, the key to understanding Executioner's Song within the context of the nonfic-tion novel genre is in another, earlier book by Mailer: Marilyn, a "biography" which appeared in 1973. The relationship between these two texts--published as "biographies"--explains how Executioner's Song fits within Norman Mailer's nonfiction work.

Packaged as a "Biography by Norman Mailer," the actual nature of the text is clear in the title of the first chapter: "A Novel Biography." Mailer's double entendre suggests that the text is actually two different works: one a fictional biography, the other a photographic collection which spans nearly all of Marilyn Monroe's life. The aesthetic space where they meet and briefly fuse into one text is in the posed quality of the photographs; just as the photographs portray a woman posing to satisfy the photographer's aesthetic conception,[22] so the fictional biography is an aesthetic gesture, a "pose" created by Norman Mailer, Novelist. Mailer actually concedes this point, indicating that much of what he distilled from Marilyn Monroe's life and legend, emerges from the following fictional hypothesis:

> Why not assume that in a family of
> such concentrated insanity as her own,
> the illegitimate daughter of Gladys
> Monroe Baker may have been born with
> a desperate imperative formed out of
> all those previous debts and failures
> of her whole family of souls.[23]

Clearly, Mailer did not construct his biography from factual information, but he rather manipulated and structured a set of preconceived interpretations built around public record: a readily available collection of personal memoirs, recollections, biographies, dates and facts.[24] Approximately one quarter of the way into the text, Mailer reveals that he fictionalized Marilyn Monroe's biography in a passage about the movie studio's reaction to the news that Monroe had just posed in the nude for a still photographer:[25]

> Now when Twentieth [Century] learns from her lips that she has, posed in the nude, <u>a novelist has a right to invent the following dialogue</u>. (92) [italics added]

Mailer's intention is clear, and the reader does not require much imagination to wonder how much of the remaining material is similarly created or "posed." In fact, this is the basis of Mailer's "biography:" <u>Marilyn</u> is an account of Marilyn Monroe's life and work reconstructed from public record[26] by a novelist who never knew her. More significant, however, is the "coincidence" between <u>Marilyn</u> and <u>Executioner's Song</u> as regards the man who is responsible for their production, Larry Schiller. Both <u>Executioner's Song</u> and <u>Marilyn</u> were contracted by Schiller who "bought the rights" to both Monroe's and Gilmore's life.[27] Mailer had no contract with Gilmore either; he was hired to complete the job of writing the book.

Thus, <u>Executioner's Song</u> clearly is also not a nonfiction novel, but is rather a conventional historical novel like Truman Capote's <u>In Cold Blood</u>. In fact, the parallels between these two crime novels go beyond the fact that both concern celebrated murders. Like <u>In Cold Blood</u>, <u>Executioner's Song</u> is narrated from an omniscient point of view which shifts between various "centres of consciousness" to provide different perspectives on the events surrounding Gary Gilmore. <u>Executioner's Song</u> is also clearly not a narrative in which Norman Mailer has a personal role (other than as implied author), and the aesthetic distance between this implied author and the narrator and characters of the novel is as great as in any conventional realistic novel. Finally, Norman Mailer, in spite of the research which obviously preceeded <u>Executioner's Song</u>, changed and exaggerated some parts of the story, for

the same reasons Capote did in In Cold Blood. Because
he used an omniscient, conventional narrator, Mailer
needed to fictionalize and typicalize certain details
in order to support the "imaginative conception" which
he drew from the Gilmore case.

Executioner's Song draws its title (and presumably
its inspiration) from a long, parodistic poem Mailer
published in an earlier text entitled Cannibals and
Christians (1966), and the authorial interpretation
drawn in the Gilmore novel partly created by the irony
generated by reading the poem and the novel by the
same name.[28]   Executioner's Song, like The Armies of
The Night, is written in two books; here the similarity
ends. The first book, "Western Voices," details the
life of Gary Gilmore from his parole from maximum
security in Marion, Illinois to a point nine months
and nine days later, when he re-enters prison for the
last time in Utah. During this period, Gilmore is
released to his cousin in Provo, Utah, and after
slightly over a month, moves away on his own and ob-
tains a full-time job. He soon meets Nicole (Baker)
Barrett, moves in with her, and after a brief period
of relative normalcy, he begins to steal, and resumes
the criminal patterns which marked his life up to this
point. After nine months, Gilmore's relationship with
Nicole breaks apart and the result, Mailer suggests,
is the murder of two young men: one in Orem, the
second in Provo. Book one ends with Gilmore's capture.

Book two, "Eastern Voices," recounts the creation
of the public Gary Gilmore, his execution, and the
subsequent developments in the lives of Nicole Barrett
and of Gilmore's mother. During this period (over
four years), Gilmore meets Larry Schiller, who nearly
becomes the major character of Book two.[29] Schiller
acquires the "rights" to Gilmore's life and tape
records hundreds of conversations between him and
Gilmore from which Executioner's Song was written.
This half of the novel also describes a different,
more intense and intellectual relationship between
Gary and Nicole and their letters, their double suicide
attempt, Gilmore's many appeals and his final success
at being executed, including the legal machinations
to prevent his execution. The novel ends with a stark
portrait of Gilmore's arthritic mother, who tried
unsuccessfully to save his life, cursing the state
from which she had come and which now had "killed my
son."

So, two portraits or "poses" of Gilmore emerge from Mailer's novel: in book one, we find a thief and hardened criminal who is barely able to stay away from trouble until he meets Nicole Baker, a woman who has a troubled and varied history of sexual encounters with men. In book two, Mailer paints a picture of the public Gary Gilmore who wants to die but can't for the "cowardly" capriciousness of the state of Utah, and who finally sells the rights to his life (and by implication, his life) to entrepreneur Larry Schiller, who becomes, ironically, a major sympathetic character in book two.

The novel is narrated from several points of view, and, from narrative section to narrative section, the narrator thinks and speaks in the language of the character whose perspective he has assumed. One of the most obvious of these shifts occurs on page 953 of the novel, where the omniscient narrator shifts from the perspective of Judy Wolbach, an angry ACLU attorney who speaks out against the Mormon legal and public majority whom she eventually holds responsible for Gary Gilmore's death, despite all of their legal efforts:

> Why Brigham Young with his countless
> wives pining on the vine had the gall
> to state that if you discovered one
> of your women in adultry, it would
> behoove you as a good and Christian
> act to hold her on your lap and run a
> knife through her breast. . . .
> Primitive Christianity! She was glad
> she'd gone to Berkeley.

to Earl Dorius, Assist. Attorney General (and a Mormon) who thinks in less graphic and angry terms than Ms. Wolbach:

> After Ms. Wolbach stopped asking
> question, Earl went over portions of
> his oral argument, then tried to get
> a little sleep. Earl was terrified.
> . . . The thought passed through his
> head, Boy if I go down and Gilmore
> lives--wouldn't that be something!
> (953-954)

Thematically, the novel plays up the blood lust of the

"primitive Christianity" which Judy Wolbach perceived to point out the irony in the state of Utah's feverish attempt to execute Gilmore in the name of "civilized" society. Technically, this device has two effects: first, it creates an immediacy used to generate suspense.[30] The reader forgets that these events have already happened and begins to conceptualize the dramatic framework of the novel in immediate terms. Thus, the events have a "timeless" quality about them. Secondly, Mailer's narrative technique emphasizes the fictional quality of the text. Practically, it would be impossible for any historian or novelist to incorporate this many different points of view into a novel and still expect the result to be an "historically accurate" text. This was true of In Cold Blood, and was one of Mailer's major arguments in The Armies of The Night. If we accept this argument, then the only plausible historical point of view is that of Norman Mailer, eye-witness, participant, and novelist, who in this case did not participate in the events of the novel. Thus, his narrative role (in Executioner's Song) is much closer to the traditional one he played in Marilyn, than to his role in The Armies of The Night.

In Executioner's Song, Mailer tries to reveal and emphasize the irony in Gary Gilmore's life and death, and one source of this irony is the contrast between the original poem "Executioner's Song" and the novel. The poem speaks of wanting to "kill well and bury well;" neither was the case with Gary Gilmore. Besides all of the embarrassing and often vigilante machinations on the part of Utah state officials to execute the man,[31] Gilmore's death at the hands of a firing squad in a prison cannery is particularly gruesome and falls far short of being "civilized" (cf. pp. 986-987). And the two lawyers, Stanger and Moody, who were given the responsibility for scattering Gilmore's ashes over Spanish Fork, Utah did so out of a used plastic bread bag, a far cry from the dignified burial Gilmore requested:

> Gary's ashes had been put into a plastic bag of the sort you sell bread in, a cellophane bag with the printing from the bread company clearly on it. (1022)

Moreover, as was already apparent in an earlier quote from Judy Wolbach, the ACLU attorney, the complicity

of the Mormon Church establishment in Gilmore's brutal
execution is suggested throughout the novel. Most of
the attorneys, prosecutors, and minor characters are
Mormons, as are the two men Gilmore killed, and in the
novel, Mailer repeatedly hints at a possible anti-
Mormon motive for Gilmore's murders.[32] In the poem
"Executioner's Song," Mailer writes:

> You see: I am bad at endings
> My bowels move without honor
> and flatulence is an affliction
> my pride must welcome with gloom.
> It comes I know from preoccupation
> much too much with sex
> those who end well do not spend
> their time so badly on the throne.[33]

The relationship between Gilmore and Nicole Baker is
initially and essentially a sexual one, and the
letters between them (especially Gary's) are explicitly
sexual, as though this were the only level of communication completely open between them.[34] In fact, both
the narrator and Gilmore (through his letters) suggest
that Gary Gilmore killed his victims because of his
breakup with Nicole, a time when Gilmore was sexually
frustrated.[35] This is supported by the passages
which imply that Gilmore may have felt uncomfortable
with male-female sexual relations, especially immediately after his parole to Provo, Utah (p. 29-30).
In addition, the Mormon church, whose polygamous past
provides an interesting background for this discussion,
is always characterized in the novel as having a
history of repressed sexuality-turned-into-bloodlust
(see quote from July Wolbach, above). Throughout the
text, Mailer develops an irony between Gilmore (who
has now become the victim of the state) and the
Mormon establishment, which now has become the blood-
thirsty killer. The irony grows from the sexually
aberrant bond Mailer sees between them; this is the
subjective perception that he (as implied author)
wishes to draw from Gary Gilmore's and Nicole Baker's
story and the design to which the historical material
in the novel is subordinated. Thus, Executioner's
Song is no different from Marilyn or In Cold Blood.
And, as in the Marilyn Monroe biography, Mailer reveals this at the end of the text.

The last page of the novel recounts a haunting
poem:

```
                    Deep in my dungeon
                    I welcome you here
                    Deep in my dungeon
                    I worship your fear
                    Deep in my dungeon,
                    I dwell.
                    I do not know
                    if I wish you well. . . . (1050)
```

which Mailer indicates is "an old prison rhyme."
However, in the afterward to the novel, Mailer admits
this is a fabrication:

> Finally, one would confess one's
> creation. The old prison rhyme at
> the beginning and end of this book
> is not, alas, an ancient ditty but
> a new one, and was written by this
> author ten years ago for his movie
> Maidstone. (1052)

And, in a second admission which throws an important
part of the novel into question, Mailer acknowledges
that the crucial passage describing the administration
of the drug Prolixin to Gilmore which might provide a
physiological clue to his homocides "has been placed
in Dr. Wood's mind with his kind permission. (1052)"
On several occasions in the novel, (pp. 400, 455, for
example), Mailer intimates that Gilmore's psychopathy
might have resulted from overadministration of the
depressant Prolixin, in much the same way that Capote
attempts to account for Perry Smith's psychopathy in
In Cold Blood, by intimating that he might suffer from
"momentary schizophrenia." The fact that he has
embellished Dr. Wood's testimony, especially, casts
much of the remaining "factual material" in Executioner's Song into doubt. In the end, Mailer's (and
Schiller's) concern was not to construct an "immaculately factual" historical account, but rather to
write a popular historical fiction which drew on well
known and "shared" material to generate the reader's
interest. Unlike The Armies of The Night which is a
nonfiction novel, Executioner's Song is a conventional
realistic novel like In Cold Blood.

[1] Hollowell, p. 90.

[2] Laura Adams, Existential Battles: _The Growth of Norman Mailer_ (Athens, Ohio: Ohio University Press, 1976), pp. 100-101).

[3] Some of these suggestions will be taken up in the conclusion of this study, Chapter Six.

[4] All three novels, it will be noted: _A Sentimental Journey. Let Us Now Praise Famous Men_, and _The Armies of The Night_, were written during similar historical periods: very intense, very confused, very emotional.

[5] Mailer facetiously dedicates _The Armies of The Night_ to LBJ, who "caused more young men and women" to read his novels.

[6] Both authors, once this period of active social participation was over, returned to writing conventional fiction: Agee in _A Death In The Family_, Mailer in _Executioner's Song_, _Marilyn_, and in his recent "magnum opus," _Ancient Mysteries_.

[7] a.) the lyrical sections, especially "On the Porch: 1,2, and 3", and b.) the more objective sections, including "Intermission: Conversation in the Lobby."

[8] Norman Mailer, _The Armies of The Night_ (New York: The New American Library, Inc., 1968), p. 14. All subsequent references will be from this edition.

[9] Agee's remarks on the subjective nature, the invented nature of journalism are useful here to understand Mailer's point, especially since the _Time_ article would be written from the perspective of the journalist.

[10] Adams, p. 130.

[11]For example, on page 37.

[12]Note that Mailer is from the start much more ironic and parodistic than Agee ever was in _Let Us Now Praise Famous Men_; in this he is much closer to Viktor Shklovsky.

[13]As with a culturally accepted myth--which is itself a "shared reality"--certain motifs seem to be part of the "reality" which the conventional reader seeks to have affirmed, and which the conventional novelist tries to reflect. For example, in the proletarian novel (American), the "starving worker" and the "greedy industrialist" are common motifs, cf. Aaron, _Writers on the Left_, Chapter one.

[14]This is the assumption behind, for example, Zola's _Le Roman Expérimental_, which deals with the novel as a shared instructive literary and scientific form. See also the important quote from Agee on pages 58-59 of this text and on page 233 of _Let Us Now Praise Famous Men_ on this problem; Agee consciously worked to avoid this "fictionalizing" in the novel in one way by identifying himself as the narrating and experiencing self in the text.

[15]This popular realistic novel has become the major market segment of American fiction sales: for example, Harold Robbins. The "sexploitive" novel has even been adopted for television, thus tapping into this large market for television viewing: e.g., H. Robbins, _The Betsy_, and Irwin Shaw, _Rich Man, Poor Man_.

[16]Throughout the novel and especially book one, Mailer tries to show the reader that there is a "media Mailer" of whom certain things are expected--and often delivered--and a "real" Norman Mailer, who is supposed to be the author and narrator of the novel. cf. page 16, for example.

[17]This is not to say that the novel is a confession by any means, but simply that there is less room for the author to become ironic or to play "games" at the expense of himself as character. This partially explains Agee's demand to know the identity and char-

107

acter of his reader; it is an almost self-defensive posture at this point.

[18]This choice in a realistic novel, Mailer suggests here, would involve selecting a "center of consciousness" who best represents the point of view the author wishes to adopt in the narrative.

[19]As had been the case in book one.

[20]This is also the point in book one which is the most lucid and existential for Mailer, since it is that moment when he must decide his actions for himself, outside any considerations of his "media self."

[21]W.F. Thrall and A. Hibbard, A Handbook to Literature (New York: The Odyssey Press, 1936), pp. 285-286. This quote also bears some relevance to the argument in this study, that the "Objective" pose of the omniscient narrator is merely a guise. The nonifction novel attempts to show and identify the "imaginative" nature of reported existence and experience.

[22]In this way she is the "raw material" of the photographer; the form of the artistic text (the photograph) is the result of his direction, lighting, camera technique, etc. And Marilyn Monroe certainly had a sense of "pose" for the camera!

[23]Norman Mailer, Marilyn (New York: Grosset & Dunlap, Inc., 1973), p. 23. All subsequent references will be from this edition.

[24]Specifically, Mailer is using the following books for much of his information, and he readily makes references to these and the fact that he is using them in this manner in the text: pp. 17, 232. Fred Lawrence Guiles, Norma Jean: The Life of Marilyn Monroe, 1968; Maurice Zolotow, Marilyn Monroe, 1960; and Norman Rosten, Marilyn--An Untold Story, 1973.

[25]Larry Schiller. This point is significant later concerning Executioner's Song.

[26]This emphasizes the fact that Mailer had no personal contact with Monroe, unlike his personal involvement in The Armies of The Night. Mailer openly cites the other texts which he is using in the narrative of Marilyn, as well.

[27]Norman Mailer, Executioner's Song (Boston: Little, Brown & Co., 1979) p. 1023.

[28]cf. for example, p. 637.

[29]We cannot help but suspect that Mailer might have had a slightly mercenary motive here, even though nothing substantial from the text could support this. In the end, Schiller could have stopped publication of the novel.

[30]Significantly, the same technique was used in Capote's novel to create the same effect. Both Mailer and Capote sought to point out the irony in the cases with which they were dealing.

[31]cf. the section on Robert Hansen, Utah Attorney General, pp. 949-956.

[32]In the text, these passages are found on the following pages: p. 463, pp. 498-499, and p. 691.

[33]Norman Mailer, Cannibals and Christians (New York: Dell Publishing Co., Inc., 1966), p. 131. Subsequent references are to this edition.

[34]cf. Gilmore's letter to Nicole on p. 478.

[35]cf. page 882. Also this is similar to the attempt which Capote made in In Cold Blood to rationalize Perry Smith's murdering lust psychologically, as a reaction to the abuses of his father and his deprived childhood.

CHAPTER SIX: CONCLUSION

One reason I so deeply care for the camera is
just this. So far as it goes (which is, in its own
realm, as absolute anyhow as the traveling distance
of words or sound), and handled cleanly and literally
in its own terms, as an ice-cold, some ways limited,
some ways more capable, eye, it is like the phonograph
record and like scientific instruments and unlike any
other leverage of art, incapable of recording anything
but absolute, dry truth.   James Agee

[Let Us Now Praise Famous Men] we might call
antidocumentary, or metaphysical documentary or
neo-Christian documentary, a form of repeated prefaces
and incidental notes to a book that cannot be written,
a form that must "fail" because, as Trilling said,
"failure alone can express the inexpressible."
W. Stott

                    *   *   *

In The Mythopoeic Reality: The Postwar American
Nonfiction Novel, Zavarzadeh recounts the following:

> Reporting that in his college library
> Agee's Let Us Now Praise Famous Men
> was shelved with the books on Alabama
> history, Samuel Hynes agrees this is
> like classifying Moby-Dick as a book
> about whales, but sympathizes with
> the librarian and declares Agee's
> book "fundamentally unclassifiable"[1]

What is most surprising about this anecdote is that
Hynes was writing in 1969, and not, say, in 1950.[2]
Until the last ten years, neither Let Us Now Praise
Famous Men's innovative structure nor its unique,
nearly poetic prose quality had "been investigated in
a systematic manner;" even outside the nonfiction
subgenre, Agee's novel "traps" even "critics who show
a special interest in a poetics of narrative. . . ."[3]
However, Agee's unique combination of personal narrative with metafictional material is more comprehensible

when we explore the text as a nonfiction novel. Doubts about whether Let Us Now Praise Famous Men is in fact a novel, as opposed to a documentary, or a journal, for example, arise only when a conventional realistic novel definition is used to explain the text. In his study on the documentary form in the United States, William Stott devotes the last portion of the text to Let Us Now Praise Famous Men, calling it "a book original to its bones; a book that undermined the period's values, cast doubt on its ideals, insulted its proprieties."4 Stott then devotes the first five pages of this last chapter to listing at least ten major differences between Agee's novel and the documentary form, and although he never calls it anything but a "book," "study," or "text," he also is clearly not comfortable with calling it a documentary, and in fact never does.5 The point is that Let Us Now Praise Famous Men, is an innovative and seminal modernist text which also happens to be a nonfiction novel. Much of our definition in Chapter One grew from a close reading of Agee's novel. Agee's repeated insistence that there is a difference between his text and the conventional realistic novel and the documentary6 indicates that Let Us Now Praise Famous Men is not a conventional novel; in fact, within the metafictional arguments are all the basic components for a new prose/nonfiction subgenre. The discussion of the nonfiction novel form in this study, it seems, has shown this, and has focused mostly on Agee's work for the same reason: Let Us Now Praise Famous Men is not only the first major American nonfiction novel, but is also an important document concerning its relationship to history and to the realistic novel.

The same, moreover, is true of Shklovsky's A Sentimental Journey, which was an equally innovative text within Russian prose literature. Shklovsky's Formalist colleagues, notwithstanding any personal attachment they might have had with Shklovsky, hailed the novel as the "start of a promising new trend in the novel" genre which "required total renewal" at the time A Sentimental Journey was published.7 Both critics, Yury Tynyanov and Boris Eichenbaum, recognized that Shklovsky's novel was a departure from the conventional novel and the memoir, but--unlike much of the critical response to Let Us Now Praise Famous Men --they also realized that A Sentimental Journey was a successive form within the novel genre. In addition, Shklovsky has continued to experiment with the non-

fiction form in Zoo, or Letters Not About Love, and
Third Factory, illustrating that the nonfiction novel
was and is still an important modernist literary form.
In American literature, the work of Norman Mailer,
especially The Armies of The Night, shows the value of
a nonfiction response to history and upheaval and
although his most recent works--Executioner's Song and
Ancient Mysteries--are not nonfiction, the three
nonfiction novels he wrote from 1965 to 1975 amply
demonstrate that this subgenre still flourishes in
the United States, as has the nonfiction work of Tom
Wolfe and Hunter S. Thompson.

In the case of American prose literature, however,
an unfortunate parallel is often drawn between Truman
Capote's In Cold Blood and the nonfiction novel: that
is, that In Cold Blood initiated the nonfiction
subgenre.[8] Clearly, this assessment is inaccurate,
since both In Cold Blood and Capote's description of
the novel are not part of the nonfiction tradition
discussed and practiced by other writers of nonfiction.
Capote's "definition" of the nonfiction novel is not
at all adequate; it is in fact a description of the
conventional realistic novel. An interesting irony
persists between Agee, Capote and Mailer as regards
In Cold Blood and Executioner's Song. When Agee
wrote Let Us Now Praise Famous Men, he came to the
novel primarily as a poet, and the poetic intensity
of much of the novel is due to this fact, as are the
passages which reveal his struggle with form and
language. In addition, there is (for Agee) an unfortunate irony in the fact that a young, idealistic,
extremely sensitive poet like James Agee should first
write a manuscript like Let Us Now Praise Famous Men
for Fortune magazine, the standard bearer of capitalism in the United States. Agee's sympathies lay
clearly with the American Left and not with mercantile
interests. Finally, Agee sought at one point not to
publish Let Us Now Praise Famous Men, feeling that the
novel's publication would "mean he had catered to the
values of his audience."[9] There is nothing mercenary
or "popular" about either Agee's subject matter or his
work within the novel.[10]

On the other hand, both Capote's In Cold Blood
and Mailer's Executioner's Song were written to take
advantage of sensational "media" events which were
given a great deal of press for a long time. Thus,
both novels were written for a "ready-made" audience,

which had already been prepared by the sensationalism which followed both the Clutter trial and the Gilmore execution. The extent to which this is a factor in Capote's novel is difficult to determine, but the circumstances surrounding Mailer's Executioner's Song would lead one to conclude that he wrote the novel expressly to take advantage of the particular readership which Gilmore's trial and execution created. The clearest distinction between these two novels and the nonfiction novel is in the relationship of the writer to the material he records in the text. While neither Capote nor Mailer had any personal or intimate connection to their subject matter (other than in research), Agee's involvement with his material is nearly too intense, too personal. The irony arises from the mistaken identification of In Cold Blood, especially, and Executioner's Song with Let Us Now Praise Famous Men as examples of nonfiction. Clearly, the narrative strength of the nonfiction novel stems from the narrator/participant's personal experience and from his struggle to prevent his individual personality from being fictionalized into the "Recording Angel" pose of conventional fiction. While the nonfictional novelist rarely if ever succeeds, he is always struggling against the "tyranny" of the fictional text.

NOTES

[1]Zavarzadeh, p. 51.

[2]cf. Samuel Hynes, "James Agee: Let Us Now Praise Famous Men," in Landmarks of American Writing, ed. by Hennig Cohen (New York: Basic Books, 1969), p. 328.

[3]Zavarzadeh, p. 51.

[4]Stott, p. 263.

[5]Ibid., pp. 290-295.

[6]In addition to echoing the claims of his later critics (such as Stott) who could not fit him into these categories.

[7]Shklovsky, A Sentimental Journey, p. xv.

[8]cf. Zavarzadeh, pp. 72n. 73, 115.

[9]Stott, p. 305n.

[10]In fact, the novel sometimes attempts the opposite.

INDEX OF NAMES

MACDONALD, Dwight: 45, 68n

MACLEISH, Archibald: 45

MAILER, Norman: 67, 87n, 88n, 89, 89-105, 113

MANN, Thomas: xii, 45

MCCLUHAN, Marshall: 22n

MOCHULSKY, Konstantin: 26n

MONAS, Sidney: 40, 43n

MONROE, Marilyn: 99-100

OHLIN, Peter: 54

OPOYAZ: 40

PELLS, Richard: xiii

PHILLIPS, William: 75

PLIMPTON, George: xv, xxn, 75

POOLE, Roger: xii

ROBBE-GRILLET, Alain: 5, 9-10, 23n, 25n

ROBBINS, Harold: 107n

ROTH, Henry: 46

SARRAUTE, Nathalie: 23n

SCHILLER, Larry: 100-101, 102

SCHOLES, Robert: 4, 22n

SHATTUCK, Roger: 22n

SHELDON, Richard: xxn, 41n

SHKLOVSKY, Victor B.: 6, 29-40, 45, 48, 79, 112

SMITH, Perry: 77

STACY, Robert: 41n

STERNE, Lawrence: 31, 40

STOTT, William: xivn, 46-47, 111

STOWE, Harriet Beecher: 13

STURROCK, John: 9, 24n

BIBLIOGRAPHY

Aaron, Daniel. _Writers on The Left_. New York: Avon
    Press, 1961.

Adams, Laura. _Existential Battles: The Growth of
    Norman Mailer_. Athens, Ohio: Ohio University
    Press, 1976.

Agee, James. _A Death In The Family_. New York: Bantam
    Books, 1969.

----------. _The Morning Watch_. New York: Bantam
    Books, 1969.

----------. _Agee On Film: Vol. 1, Reviews and
    Comments_. Boston: Beacon Press, 1960.

----------. _Agee On Film: Vol. 2, Five Film Scripts_.
    Boston: Beacon Press, 1960.

----------. _The Letters of James Agee to Father Flye_.
    New York: Bantam Books, 1963.

----------. "Art For What's Sake." _The New Masses_,
    21, No. 12 (1936) pp. 48-50.

----------. "Comedy's Greatest Era." _Life_, 27 (1949)
    pp. 70-88.

----------. "Self-Portrait." _Esquire_, 60 (1963)
    p. 149.

----------, and Walker Evans. _Let Us Now Praise
    Famous Men_. Boston: Houghton-Mifflin Co., 1961.

Bakhtin, Mikhail. _Problems of Dostoevsky's Poetics_.
    Ann Arbor: Ardis Publishers, 1973.

Bann, Stephen, and John E. Bowlt, eds. _Russian
    Formalism: A Collection of Articles and Texts in
    Translation_. New York: Harper & Row, 1973.

Barnouw, Erik. _Documentary: A History of the Non-
    Fiction Film_. New York: Oxford University Press,
    1974.

Barson, Alfred T. A Way of Seeing: A Critical Study
  of James Agee. Amherst: University of Massachu-
  setts Press, 1972.

Barzun, Jacques. "Proust's Way." The Griffin 5
  (1956) pp. 4-13.

Behar, Jack. "James Agee: The World of His Work."
  Diss. Ohio State, 1963.

Bennett, Tony. Formalism and Marxism. London:
  Metheun, 1979.

Black, Edwin. Rhetorical Criticism: A Study In
  Method. Madison: University of Wisconsin Press,
  1978.

Blake, Patricia, and Max Hayward, eds. Dissonant
  Voices in Soviet Literature. New York: Random
  House, 1962.

Booth, Wayne. The Rhetoric of Fiction. Chicago:
  University of Chicago Press, 1971.

Bufethis, Philip H. Norman Mailer. New York:
  Frederick Ungar Publishers, 1978.

Butor, Michel. "Interview With Michel Butor." In
  Direction in The Noveau Roman. Ed. G. Almansi,
  Canterbury, U.K.: Scottish Academic Press, 1971,
  pp. 41-52.

Capote, Truman. In Cold Blood. New York: Random
  House, 1965.

Chase, Richard. The American Novel and Its Tradition.
  New York: Doubleday & Co., 1957.

Chesnick, Eugene. "The Plot Against Fiction: Let Us
  Now Praise Famous Men." The Southern Literary
  Journal, (1971), pp. 48-67.

Cheuse, Alan. "The Return of James Agee." The New
  York Times Magazine, 16 December 1979, pp. 12-46.

Clark, Katerina. The Soviet Novel: History As Ritual.
  Chicago: University of Chicago Press, 1981.

Coles, R. Irony in The Mind's Life. Richmond, Va.:
    University Press of Virginia, 1976.

Cowley, Malcolm. And I Worked at The Writer's Trade.
    New York: The Viking Press, 1978.

Culler, Jonathan. "Fabula and Sjuzhet in The Analysis
    of Narrative: Some American Discussion." Poetics
    Today, 1, No. 3 (1980) pp. 27-38.

De Voto, Bernard. "The Invisible Novelist." In The
    World of Fiction. Boston: Little, Brown, 1950,
    pp. 58-81.

Deležel, Lubomír. "Truth and Authenticity in Narra-
    tive." Poetics Today, 1, No. 3 (1980) pp. 7-26.

Dunham, Vera S. In Stalin's Time: Middleclass Values
    in Soviet Fiction. Cambridge: Cambridge Univer-
    sity Press, 1979.

Eagleton, Terry. Literary Theory. Minneapolis:
    University of Minnesota Press, 1983.

Erlich, Victor. Russian Formalism: History and De-
    cline. The Hague: Mouton & Company, 1965.

Euripides. "Heracles." In Euripides I. Ed. by
    David Greene and Richard Lattimore. New York:
    Random House, 1956.

Field, Andrew, ed. The Complection of Russian Liter-
    ature. New York: Atheneum, 1971.

Fitzgerald, Robert, ed. The Collected Prose of James
    Agee. New York: Ballantine Books, 1968.

----------. "A Memoir." In The Collected Prose of
    James Agee. Ed. by Robert Fitzgerald. New York:
    Ballantine Books, 1968, pp. 3-66.

Fletcher, Angus, Ed. The Literature of Fact: Selected
    Papers From the English Institute. New York:
    Columbia University Press, 1976.

Fletcher, John and Malcolm Bradbury. "The Introverted
    Novel," In Modernism. Ed. by Malcolm Bradbury
    and James MacFarlane. Middlesex, U.K.: Penquin
    Books, Ltd., 1976, pp. 394-415.

Foster, Richard. _Norman Mailer_. Minneapolis:
     University of Minnesota Press, 1968.

Friedman, Norman. "Point of View In Fiction." In
     The Theory of the Novel. Ed. by Philip Stevick.
     New York: The Free Press, 1967, pp. 108-137.

Fuller, Edmund. _Man In Modern Fiction: Some Minority
     Opinions On Contemporary American Writing_. New
     York: Random House, 1958.

Gibian, George, and H. W. Tjalsma, eds. _Russian
     Modernism: Culture and The Avant-Garde, 1900-
     1930_. Ithaca: Cornell University Press, 1976.

Grant, Damian. _Realism_. London: Methuen & Co., Ltd.,
     1970

Grits, Fyodor S. "The Work of Viktor Shklovsky, An
     Analysis of _Third Factory_." In _Third Factory_.
     Ed. by Richard Sheldon. Ann Arbor: Ardis, 1977,
     pp. 91-121.

Gutman, Stanley T. _Mankind In Barbary. The Indivi-
     dual and Society in the Novels of Norman Mailer_.
     New Hampshire: The University Press of New
     England, 1975.

Habermas, Jürgen. _Communication and the Evolution of
     Society_. Trans. by Thomas McCarthy. Boston:
     Beacon Press, 1979.

Halperin, John, ed. _The Theory of the Novel: New
     Essays_. New York: Oxford University Press, 1974.

Heidsieck, Arnold. _Das Groteske Und das Absurde in
     modernen Drama_. Stuttgart: Kohlhammer, 1969.

Hellmann, John. _Fables of Fact: The New Journalism
     As New Fiction_. Urbana: University of Illinois
     Press, 1981.

Hersey, John. _The Algiers Motel Incident_. New York:
     Knopf, 1968.

Hirsch, E.D. _The Aims of Interpretation_. Chicago:
     University of Chicago Press, 1976.

Hollowell, John. _Fact and Fiction: The New Journalism_
and The Nonfiction Novel. Chapel Hill, N.C.:
University of North Carolina Press, 1977.

James, Henry. _The Art of the Novel: Critical Prefaces_
by Henry James. Ed. by R.P. Blackmur. New York:
Charles Scribner's Sons, 1937.

Jameson, Fredric. _The Prison-House of Language_.
Princeton: Princeton University Press, 1972.

Kaminsky, Alice R. "On Literary Realism." In _The_
Theory of the Novel: New Essays. Ed. by John
Halperin. New York: Oxford University Press,
1974, pp. 213-231.

Karlinsky, Simon, and Alfred Appel, eds. _The Bitter_
Air of Exile: Russian Writers in The West,
1922-1972, Berkeley: University of California
Press, 1973.

Kaufmann, Donald C. _Norman Mailer, The Countdown:_
The First Twenty Years. Carbondale: Southern
Illinois University Press, 1969.

Kazin, Alfred. _Starting Out In The Thirties_. New
York: Random House, 1980.

Kermode, Frank. "Institutional Control of Interpretation." _Salmagundi_ 43: Winter 1979, pp. 72-86.

Kinneavy, James. _A Theory of Discourse_. New Jersey:
Prentice-Hall, 1971.

Larson, Erling. _James Agee_. Minneapolis: University
of Minnesota Press, 1971.

Levin, Harry. _The Gates of Horn: A Study of Five_
French Realists. New York: Oxford University
Press, 1963.

Levine, George. "Realism Reconsidered." In _The_
Theory of the Novel: New Essays. Ed. by John
Halperin. New York: Oxford University Press,
1974, pp. 233-255.

Lindstrom, Thais S. _A Concise History of Russian_
Literature From 1900 to the Present. New York:
New York University Press, 1978.

Linner, Sven. <u>Dostoevskij on Realism</u>. Stockholm
    Slavic Studies. 1 (1967).

Lodge, David. "The Language of Modernist Fiction:
    Metaphor and Metonymy." In <u>Modernism</u>. Ed. by
    Malcolm Bradbury and James MacFarlane. Middle-
    sex, U.K.: Penguin Books, Ltd., 1976, pp. 481-496.

----------. "The Novelist At The Crossroads." In <u>The
    Novel Today</u>. Ed. by Malcolm Bradbury. Rowan:
    Manchester University Press, 1977, pp. 84-110.

Loofbourrow, John W. "Realism in the Anglo-American
    Novel: The Pastoral Myth." In <u>The Theory of The
    Novel: New Essays</u>. Ed. by John Halperin. New
    York: Oxford University Press, 1974, pp. 257-269.

Lowenkron, David Henry. "The Metanovel." <u>College
    English</u> 38:4 December 1976, pp. 343-355.

Lucid, Robert F. <u>Norman Mailer: The Man and His Work</u>.
    Boston: Little, Brown & Co., 1971.

Lukács, György. <u>Die Theorie des Romans: ein
    geschichtsphilosophischer Versuch über die Formen
    der grossen Epik</u>. Neuwied: Luchterhand, 1963.

----------. <u>Probleme des Realismus</u>. Neuwied:
    Luchterhand, 1971.

MacDonald, Dwight. "Jim Agee, A Memoir." In <u>Remem-
    bering James Agee</u>. Ed. by David Madden. Baton
    Rouge: Louisiana State University Press, 1974,
    pp. 103-107.

Madden, David, ed. <u>Proletarian Writers of the
    Thirties</u>. Carbondale: Southern Illinois Univer-
    sity Press, 1968.

----------. <u>Tough Guy Writers of the Thirties</u>.
    Carbondale: Southern Illinois University Press,
    1967.

----------. <u>Remembering James Agee</u>. Baton Rouge:
    Louisiana State University Press, 1974.

Mailer, Norman. <u>Existential Errands</u>. Boston: Little
    Brown, and Company, 1972.

----------. Executioner's Song. Boston: Little, Brown, and Company, 1979.

----------. Marilyn. New York: Grosset & Dunlap, Inc., 1973.

----------. The Armies of The Night. New York: The New American Library, Inc., 1968.

----------. St. George and the Godfather. New York: The New American Library, 1972.

----------. Of A Fire On The Moon. New York: The New American Library, 1969.

----------. Cannibals and Christians. New York: Dell Publishing Co., Inc., 1966.

----------. Miami and the Siege of Chicago: An Informal History of the Republican and Democratic Conventions of 1968. New York: The World Publishing Company, 1968.

----------. Norman Mailer: A Collection of Critical Essays. Ed. by Leo Brandy. New Jersey: Prentice-Hall, Inc., 1972.

----------. The Long Patrol: 25 Years of Writing From the Work of Norman Mailer. Ed. by Robert F. Lucid. New York: World Publishing Co., 1971.

----------. Genius and Lust: A Journey Through the Major Writings of Henry Miller. New York: Grove Press, Inc., 1976.

Malin, Irving, ed. Truman Capote's In Cold Blood: A Critical Handbook. Belmont, Cal.: Wadsworth Publishing, 1968.

Mann, Thomas. Doktor Faustus. Frankfurt am Main: Fischer Bücherei, 1967.

McCluhan, Marshall. The Medium is The Massage. New York: Goddard University Press, 1969.

Mercier, Vivian. The New Novel: From Queneau to Pinget. New York: Farrar, Straus and Giroux, 1971.

Merrill, Robert. _Norman Mailer_. Boston: Twayne
    Publishers, 1978.

Mochulsky, Konstantin. _Dostoevsky: His Life and Work_.
    Trans. by M. A. Minihan. Princeton: Princeton
    University Press, 1973.

Monas, Sidney. "Driving Nails With a Samovar: A
    Historical Introduction." In _A Sentimental
    Journey_. Trans. by Richard Sheldon. Ithaca:
    Cornell University Press, 1970.

Moreau, Geneviève. _The Restless Journey of James
    Agee_. Trans. by Miriam Kleiger. New York:
    William Morrow and Company, 1977.

Neuberg, Victor E. _Popular Literature: A History and
    Guide_. Middlesex, U.K.: Penguin Books, Ltd,
    1977.

North, Joseph, ed. _The New Masses: An Anthology_. New
    York: International Publishers, 1971.

Ohlin, Peter H. _Agee_. New York: Ivan Obolensky,
    Inc., 1966.

Ortega Y Gasset, José. _The Dehumanization of Art and
    Notes On the Novel_. Trans. by Helene Weyl.
    Princeton: Princeton University Press, 1948.

Peace, Richard. _Dostoevsky: An Examination of the
    Major Novels_. Cambridge: Cambridge University
    Press, 1970.

Pells, Richard. _Radical Visions and American Dreams:
    Culture and Thought in the Depression Years_.
    New York: Harper & Row, 1973.

Plimpton, George. "The Story Behind a Nonfiction
    Novel." In _Truman Capote's In Cold Blood: A
    Critical Handbook_. Ed. by Irving Malin.
    Belmont, Calif.: Wadsworth Publishing Co., 1969,
    pp. 25-43.

Poirier, Richard. _Norman Mailer_. New York: The
    Viking Press, 1972.

Pomorska, Krystyna. _Russian Formalist Theory and It's
    Poetic Ambiance_. The Hague: Monton, 1968.

Rebel America: The Story of Social Revolt in the
    United States. Boston: Beacon Press, 1972

Rideout, Walter. The Radical Novel in the United
    States, 1900-1954. Cambridge, Mass.: Harvard
    University Press, 1956.

Robbe-Grillet, Alain. La Jalousie. Paris: Les
    Éditions de Minuit, 1957.

Rühle, Jürgen. Literature and Revolution: A Critical
    Study of the Writer and Communism in the Twen-
    tieth Century. Ed. by Jean Steinberg. New York:
    Frederick A. Praeger Publishing, 1969.

Sarraute, Nathalie. L'Ère du soupcon: essais sur le
    roman. Paris: Gallimard, 1956.

----------. Telephone Interview. 14 November 1977.

Scholes, Robert. Fabulation and Metafiction. Urbana:
    University of Illinois Press, 1979.

----------. "The Contributions of Formalism and
    Structuralism to the Theory of Fiction." In
    Towards a Poetics of Fiction. Ed. by Mark
    Spilka. Bloomington: Indiana University Press,
    1977, pp. 176-211.

Schramke, Jürgen. Zur Theorie des modernen Romans.
    München: C.H. Beck, 1976

Seib, Kenneth. James Agee: Promise and Fulfillment.
    Pittsburgh: University of Pittsburgh Press, 1968.

Stattuck, Roger. The Banquet Years. New York: Dutton
    & Co., 1967.

Sheldon, Richard. Shklovsky: An International Biblio-
    graphy of Works by and About Him. Ann Arbor:
    Ardis, 1977.

----------. "Viktor Shklovsky and the Device of
    Ostensible Surrender." In Third Factory. Ed.
    and trans. by Richard Sheldon. Ann Arbor: Ardis,
    1977, pp. vi-xxvii.

----------. "Viktor Borisovič Shklovsky: Literary
    Theory and Practice, 1914-1930." Diss. Univer-
    sity of Michigan, 1966.

Sherwood, Richard. "Viktor Shklovsky and the Develop-
    ment of Early Formalist Theory on Prose Litera-
    ture." In Russian Formalism: A Collection of
    Articles and Texts In Translation. Ed. by
    Stephen Bann and John E. Bowalt. New York:
    Harper & Row, 1973, pp. 47-56.

Sherzer, Dina. "Serial Constructs in the Nouveau
    Roman." Poetics Today. 1, No. 3 (1980) pp. 87-
    106.

Shklovsky, Viktor B. A Sentimental Journey. Trans. by
    Richard Sheldon. Ithaca: Cornell University
    Press, 1970.

----------. O teorii prozy. Moscow: n.p., 1929.

----------. Theorie der Prosa. (1925 edition) Trans.
    by Gisela Drohla. Frankfurt am Main: S. Fischer
    Verlap GmbH, 1966.

----------. "La Construction de la Nouvelle et du
    Roman." In Théorie de la Littérature. Ed. by
    Tzvetan Todorov. Paris: Edition de Seuil, 1965,
    pp. 170-196.

----------. Zoo, or Letters Not About Love. Trans.
    and ed. by Richard Sheldon. Ithaca: Cornell
    University Press, 1971

----------. Lev Tolstoy, Trans. by Olga Shartse.
    Moscow: Progress Publishers, 1978.

----------. "Viktor Shklovsky on Isaac Babel." In
    The Complection of Russian Literature. Ed. by
    Andrew Field. New York: Atheneim, 1971, pp. 203-
    207.

----------. "Viktor Shklovsky on Leo Tolstoy." In
    The Complection of Russian Literature. Ed. by
    Andrew Field. New York: Atheneim, 1971, pp.
    125-131.

----------. "The Resurrection of the Word." In
    Russian Formalism: A Collection of Articles and

Texts in Translation. Ed. by Stephen Bann and
John E. Bowlt. New York: Harper & Row, 1973,
pp. 67-90.

----------. Mayakovsky and His Circle. Trans. and
ed. by Lily Feiler. New York: Dodd, Mead, & Co.,
1972.

----------. "Art as Technique." In Russian Formalist
Criticism: Four Essays. Trans. and ed. by Lee
T. Lemon and Marion J. Reis. Lincoln, Neb.:
University of Nebraska Press, 1965, pp. 10-28.

----------. "Sterne's Tristram Shandy: Stylistic
Commentary." In Russian Formalist Criticism:
Four Essays. Trans. and ed. by Lee T. Lemon and
Marion J. Reis. Lincoln, Neb.: University of
Nebraska Press, 1965, pp. 30-49.

----------. "Form and Material In Art." In Dissonant
Voices in Soviet Literature. Ed. by Patricia
Blake and Max Hayward. New York: Random House,
1962, pp. 20-28.

----------. Pro and Contra. Remarks on Dostoevsky.
Moscow: n.p., 1957.

----------. Third Factory. Trans. by Richard Sheldon
Ann Arbor: Ardis Press, 1977.

----------. "L'Art Comme Procédé." In Théorie de la
Littérature. Ed. and Trans. by Tzvetan Todorov.
Paris: Editions du Seuil, 1965, pp. 76-97.

Simon, Rita James. ed. As We Saw The Thirties: Essays
on Social and Political Movements of a Decade.
Urbana: University of Illinois Press, 1967.

Smart, Robert A. "The Rhetoric of the Grotesque:
Edgar A. Poe and Franz Kafka." Thesis University
of Utah, 1977.

Snodgrass, W.D. In Radical Pursuit. New York: Harper
& Row, 1975.

Solotaroff, Robert. Down Mailer's Way. Urbana:
University of Illinois Press, 1974.

Spender, Stephen. The '30's and After: Poetry, Poli-
     tics, People, 1930's-1970's. New York: Random
     House, 1978.

Spilka, Mark, ed. Towards a Poetics of Fiction.
     Bloomington: Indiana University Press, 1977.

Stacy, Robert H. Defamiliarization in Language and
     Literature. New York: Syracuse University Press,
     1977.

Stanzel, Franz K. Typische Formen des Romans.
     Göttingen: Vandenhoeck & Ruprecht, 1964.

Sternberg, Meir. Expositional Modes and Temporal
     Ordering in Fiction. Baltimore: The John Hopkins
     University Press, 1978.

Stott, William. Documentary Expression and Thirties
     America. New York: Oxford University Press,
     1973.

Stovall, Floyd A. The Development of American Liter-
     ary Criticism. New Haven: College and University
     Press, 1955.

Straumann, Heinrich. American Literature in the
     Twentieth Century. New York: Harper & Row, 1965.

Struve, Gleb. Russian Literature Under Lenin and
     Stalin, 1917-1952. Norman: University of Okla-
     homa Press, 1971.

Sturrock, John. "The project of a l'aine robe
     grillée." In Directions in the Nouveau Roman.
     Ed. G. Almansi. Canterbury, U.K.: Scottish
     Academic Press, 1971, pp. 6-16.

Susman, Warren I. "The Thirties." In The Development
     of an American Culture. Ed. by Stanley Coben and
     Lorman Ratner. New Jersey: Prentice Hall, Inc.,
     1970, pp. 179-218.

Sypher, Wylie. Loss of the Self in Modern Literature
     and Art. New York: Random House, 1962.

Tanner, Tony. "On the Parapet." In Will The Real
     Norman Mailer Please Stand Up. Ed. by Laura
     Adams. Port Washington, N.Y.: Kennikat Press,
     1974, pp. 47-62

Tar, Zoltán. The Frankfurt School. New York: John
    Wiley and Sons, 1977.

Terkel, Studs, ed. Hard Times: An Oral History of The
    Great Depression. New York: Avon Books, 1970.

Terras, Victor. Belinskij and Russian Literary Cri-
    ticism: The Heritage of Organic Aesthetics.
    Madison: University of Wisconsin Press, 1974.

Thrall, W.F., and A. Hibbard. A Handbook to
    Literature. New York: The Odyssey Press, 1936.

Todorov, Tzvetan, ed. Théorie de la Littérature.
    Paris: Édition du Seuil, 1965.

Tompkins, Phillip K. "In Cold Fact." In Truman
    Capote's In Cold Blood: A Critical Handbook. Ed.
    by Irving Malin. Belmont, Cal.: Wadsworth
    Publishing Co., 1968, pp. 44-58.

Trilling, Diana. "Capote's Crime and Punishment."
    Partisan Review 33, No. 1 (1966) pp. 252-259.

Trilling, Lionel. The Liberal Imagination. New York:
    Oxford University Press, 1950.

Volpe, Galvano Della. "Settling Accounts with The
    Russian Formalists." The New Left Review 113-
    114 (1979) pp. 133-145.

Watt, Ian. The Rise of The Novel. Berkeley: Univer-
    sity of California Press, 1957.

Weber, Ronald. The Literature of Fact. Athens, Ohio:
    Ohio University Press, 1980.

----------. Ed. The Reporter As Artist. New York:
    Hastings House, 1974.

Wellek, René, and Austin Warren. Theory of Litera-
    ture. New York: Harcourt, Brace & World, 1956.

----------. "Russian Formalism." In Russian
    Modernism: Culture and the Avant Garde, 1900-
    1930. Ed. by George Gibian and H.W. Tjalsma.
    Ithaca: Cornell University Press, 1976, pp. 58-69.

White, Hayden. "The Fictions of Factual Representation." In The Literature of Fact. Ed. by Angus Fletcher. New York: Columbia University Press, 1976.

Wilson, Edmund. To the Finland Station: A Study in the Writing and Acting of History. Garden City: Doubleday and Co., 1940.

----------. The Shores of Light: A Literary Chronicle of the '20's and '30's. New York: Farrar, Straus & Giroux, 1952.

----------. The Twenties. Ed. by Leon Edel. New York: Farrar, Straus & Giroux, 1975.

Wish, Harvey, ed. Ante-bellum: Three Classic Works on Slavery in the Old South by Hinton Rowan Helper and George Fitzhugh. New York: G.P. Putnam's Sons, Ltd., 1960.

Woodcock, George. "When The Past Becomes History: The Century in Non-Fiction Prose." University of Toronto Quarterly 50, No. 1 (1980) pp. 90-101.

Zavarzadeh, Mas'ud. The Mythopoeic Reality: The Postwar American Nonfiction Novel. Urbana: University of Illinois Press, 1976.

Robert A. Smart is a native of Maine, and received his Ph.D. from the University of Utah in Comparative Literature in 1980. He has taught at The University of Maine at Fort Kent, at Westminster College, and is now at Bradford College, Bradford, Mass. He is also the editor in chief of <u>The Writing Teacher</u>.